PATTERNS OF COSTA RICAN POLITICS

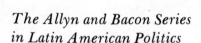

The Allyn and Bacon Series
in Latin American Politics

FEDERICO G. GIL, EDITOR
THE UNIVERSITY OF NORTH CAROLINA

ARPAD VON LAZAR, ASSOCIATE EDITOR
THE FLETCHER SCHOOL OF LAW AND DIPLOMACY
TUFTS UNIVERSITY

ALLYN AND BACON, INC.   BOSTON

Patterns of Costa Rican Politics

CHARLES F. DENTON
Wayne State University

LIBRARY OF CONGRESS CATALOG CARD NUMBER: 76-116571
PRINTED IN THE UNITED STATES OF AMERICA

Acknowledgments

No work of this type can be carried out singlehandedly. A great number of people usually contribute in a variety of ways; typing, editing, advising, funding, and providing moral support. The effort which this book represents is no exception. To name everyone worthy of mention would bring forth the wrath of the publishers and editors.

Milton Clarke, Alvaro Vega, Alejandro Karpinsky, Francisco Cordero, and Charles Troutman all rendered invaluable assistance on the field in Costa Rica, where the author conducted research in 1967–68 with the help of a Fulbright-Hays Scholarship. Professors Charles J. Parrish and Karl Schmitt of the Department of Government of the University of Texas read earlier versions of this manuscript and provided well-deserved critical comments. Chris Baker of the Department of Political Science at the University of Florida devoted many hours of his valuable time discussing some of the ideas presented herein with the author. Patrick Henry of the Panama Canal Company prepared two of the graphs in the book. To Professor Federico Gil of the Institute of Latin American Studies at the University of North Carolina goes a special word of thanks for suggestions as to how to make an improbable manuscript into a probable book.

Without the moral and financial support of my parents, Mr. and Mrs. Fred L. Denton, this project would never have been started. Louise, Freddy, and Mark have demonstrated great patience with their husband and father in recent years, but it is to Louise to whom this work is dedicated.

It should go without saying that all errors, omissions, or faults in this small volume are exclusively the responsibility of the author.

C.F.D.

Contents

Preface

Peaceful, small in territory and population, economically weak, Costa Rica has hardly played a noticeable role in the conduct of world affairs. In fact, for many years journalists, and even scholars, referred to the Central American nation simply as one of the "banana" republics. Social scientists have generally neglected it, giving larger and more politically turbulent countries in the Latin American area a higher research priority. Almost no empirically oriented research of a political nature has been conducted in Costa Rica; of the very few political science studies carried out there, virtually all have been institutionally oriented and normative in nature.[1] And yet the country has frequently been classed by North American analysts as one of the more politically developed nations in the Western Hemisphere.[2]

This book does not pretend to provide a one-volume, comprehensive analysis of the Costa Rican political process, but instead is designed to be an introductory background, partially filling some of the larger gaps in the information available about the country. Even such a tiny nation as this one is sufficiently complex to require much more attention than it receives here.

Political analyst Fred W. Riggs has noted that in transitional societies such as Costa Rica there are usually no distinct boundaries between the political process on the one hand, and the economic,

[1] Two exceptions are Daniel Goldrich, *Sons of the Establishment: Elite Youth in Panama and Costa Rica* (Chicago: Rand McNally, 1966), and John D. Martz, "Costa Rican Electoral Trends, 1953–1966," *Western Political Quarterly* 20, No. 4 (December, 1967), 888–909.

[2] Among the analysts who have labeled Costa Rica as highly developed within the Latin American context are: Russell H. Fitzgibbon, "Measuring Democratic Change in Latin America," *Journal of Politics* 29, No. 1 (February, 1967), 129–65; Martin C. Needler, "Political Development and Socioeconomic Development: The Case of Latin America," *American Political Science Review* 62, No. 3 (September, 1968), 889–97; "Costa Rica: A Progressing Democracy," in Harry Kantor, *Patterns of Politics and Political Systems in Latin America* (Chicago: Rand McNally, 1969), pp. 187–225.

social, and cultural processes on the other hand.[3] In noting this overlap Riggs has called for a "pan-disciplinarian" approach to the analysis of social phenomena in nations of this type. Following the lead of Riggs and other social scientists, this analysis first focuses on the various environments of the Costa Rican political process and their relation to it. Of course, the central focus of this work is the conduct of politics itself.

When a "pan-disciplinarian" approach to the study of social phenomena is used, a question can be reasonably posed as to why there should be a particular emphasis on politics. To a certain extent, such an emphasis merely reflects the particular discipline of the social scientist conducting the study. But, as Alfred Diamant notes in a recent article, in the transitional societies in particular, the political apparatus becomes the chief locus of decision making and problem solving.[4] Few major decisions of any type—decisions which affect a sizeable portion of the upper social sectors—are made outside of the political arena. This is true even if the decisions appear to have been taken about matters with little or no political content: for example, what type of industry will locate in a country or whether or not a national symphonic orchestra will survive another year. At the same time few political decisions are made which do not affect other societal arenas as well. In short, to ignore the various environments of the Costa Rican political process would be to detract significantly from the usefulness of this study.

The organizing concept of this analysis is that of politics as a system, but, as should be clear from the above, a system which virtually overlaps with other Costa Rican social systems and which has boundaries that are indistinguishable in most cases from them.[5] Political processes are viewed as being functional to the system, while particular emphasis is placed on the capability of the political system to sustain change for the society as a whole.

[3] Fred W. Riggs, *Administration in Developing Countries* (Boston: Houghton Mifflin Company, 1964), pp. 52–54.

[4] Alfred Diamant, "The Nature of Political Development," in Jason L. Finkle and Richard W. Gable (eds.), *Political Development and Social Change* (New York: John Wiley and Sons, Inc., 1966), p. 91.

[5] Many of the concepts used here have been adapted from Gabriel A. Almond and G. Bingham Powell, Jr., *Comparative Politics: A Developmental Approach* (Boston: Little, Brown and Company, 1966).

1

The Class Structure
and Social Mobilization

Costa Rica's human resources are expanding as fast as those of any country in the world. Between 1950 and 1966, for example, the average annual population growth rate was 3.7 percent.[1] Considering biological limitations it is virtually impossible for a population to grow much more rapidly than this. At the 1950–66 rate it is estimated that the population of Costa Rica, which amounted to some 1,463,013 persons in 1965, will reach approximately 3,493,265 by 1990.[2] In other words the population will come short of tripling in a matter of twenty-five years. This rapid growth rate has had profound effects on the socioeconomic and political systems of the country.

A principal effect of the population growth rate in Costa Rica has been the limitations the increases have imposed on per capita income growth rates and the money economy. As a result of the 3.7 percent growth rate in the nation's human resources, per capita income grows at a low annual average 1.6 percent, and between 1958 and 1962 it actually decreased.[3] With almost half of its population under the age of fifteen and still inactively economically, Costa Rica cannot have much hope for a rapid per capita income

[1] Presidencia de la República, Oficina de Planificación, *Cuadra de análisis de los principales variables económicos y sociales* (San José, 1967), p. 5.

[2] Dirección General de Estadística y Censo, *Proyección de la población de Costa Rica por sexos y grupos de edad, 1965–1990* (San José, 1967), p. 4.

[3] Oficina de Planificación, *Características de la economía de Costa Rica, 1950–1962*, p. 29.

increase in the near future. Further accentuating the problem is the
fact that out of 386,990 females over the age of twelve in the total
population, only 16 percent are employed and the birth rate among
the unemployed women is double that of those who do work.[4]

Population Concentration

Most visitors to Costa Rica come away with the impression of
a highly mountainous country characterized by valleys and plateaus
and clustered with brightly painted villages not very distant from
each other. This is a fairly accurate picture of the nonurban areas
of the country's central plateau, the region seen by the majority of
visitors to the exclusion of all others. This is also the region regarded by most Costa Ricans as typical of their country; it is like-
wise the place where most of them wish to reside.

The central plateau, an expanse of some four thousand square
kilometers (2500 square miles) or approximately 8 percent of the
total national land area, contains almost 60 percent of Costa Rica's
population. Residing on this plateau are 80 percent of the work
force; 79 percent of all hospital beds and some 83 percent of total
national capital investment are to be found in this region.[5] This
situation has operated to the disadvantage of the rest of the country.
For example, though Costa Rica has an official literacy rate of 85
percent—one of the highest in Latin America—85 percent of the
illiterates live *outside* of the central plateau area, where schools
are not as accessible and communications are more limited.[6]

Costa Rican statistics reveal that urban population areas have
been growing at an annual rate of 4.3 percent, some .6 percent
faster than the population as a whole.[7] At first glance this would
hardly seem to be problematical, particularly if urbanization figures
for other Latin American countries are examined. In 1963 the country was only 34 percent urban; however, it is the concentration in
the central plateau which is problematical. The great majority of
all economic and social infrastructure is centered in this area, to

[4] Oficina de Planificación, *La economía de Costa Rica en 1966*, p. 67.

[5] Ibid., pp. 21–23.

[6] Dirreción General de Estadística y Censo, *Censo de población, 1963*, p. 474.

[7] *La economía de Costa Rica en 1966*, p. 21.

the almost total neglect of other regions of the country. Yet it is on the areas away from the central plateau that Costa Rica depends for growing most of its cash crops to export and thus provide economic growth; it is on the staple foodstuffs grown away from the central plateau that the country depends to feed most of its population. But until the Costa Rican political system begins to allocate resources and infrastructure to areas away from San José and its environs, it is improbable that people in greater numbers will be willing to live in those areas.

Social Mobility

Rapid population growth rates have severely taxed Costa Rican educational facilities. As Graph 1 shows, only a small percentage of those entering the first grade in public and private schools manage to complete high school; an even smaller group obtains a university education. It must be pointed out, however, that virtually the entire population does enter the first grade, a feat matched by few Latin American countries. All but a few Costa Ricans do obtain the rudiments of reading and writing.

Aldo Solari has written that in Costa Rica, almost unique in Latin America, lower middle-class and working-class children are able to attend academic schools preparing them for university.[8] However, Graph 1 indicates that the situation is other than the one suggested by Solari. For if only 5 percent of the population completes high school, then it would seem probable that few students of working-class origin ever do enter secondary school to prepare for university. And there is a definite social barrier between the last year of high school and the first year of university. There is only one university in the entire country, and it is located in San José on the central plateau. Assuming that students from other areas of the country are able to complete their secondary education in one of the few high schools outside of the central plateau, they must possess sufficient resources to permit a move to San José to attend the university there. The university annually has a limited number of openings in its first year due to limitations

[8] Aldo Solari, "Secondary Education and the Development of Elites," in Seymour M. Lipset and Aldo Solari (eds.), *Elites in Latin America* (New York: Oxford University Press, 1967), p. 468.

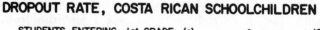

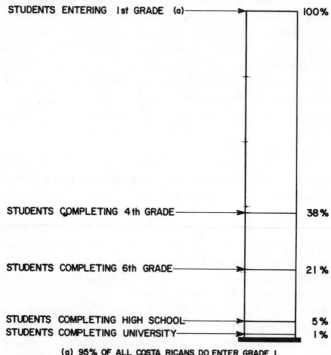

Graph 1

DROPOUT RATE, COSTA RICAN SCHOOLCHILDREN

STUDENTS ENTERING 1st GRADE (a) ——————→ 100%

STUDENTS COMPLETING 4th GRADE ——————→ 38%

STUDENTS COMPLETING 6th GRADE ——————→ 21%

STUDENTS COMPLETING HIGH SCHOOL ——————→ 5%
STUDENTS COMPLETING UNIVERSITY ——————→ 1%

(a) 95% OF ALL COSTA RICANS DO ENTER GRADE I.

SOURCE: CENSO DE POBLACIÓN, PP. 510-518

imposed by a shortage of trained professors and physical plant. There are never sufficient openings for the number of persons completing high school. For the academic year beginning in March, 1968, for example, the University of Costa Rica received five thousand applications for admission from qualified students to the first year. Only 2,600 students, slightly over half of the applications, were actually admitted.

Further weakening Solari's argument are the results of matriculation examinations taken by 1967 high school graduates. Out of 5,716 secondary school graduates in that year only 2,517 were capable of passing the examinations. Of the graduates from private, usually parochial, high schools taking this examination, 69 percent were able to pass as compared to only 47 percent of the students who completed their education in high schools run by the government. However, passing the exam does not assure admission to the university, for there is usually a backlog of approximately five thousand students on a waiting list from earlier years. These students passed the exam previously and were not admitted simply because space for them was lacking.

Wealthier Costa Rican families sidestep this problem by sending their children abroad, usually to the United States, to obtain higher degrees. These students, regardless of academic qualifications, avoid waiting several years after high school graduation to begin attending a university, and usually they assume a more prestigious position upon returning from abroad. This situation further accentuates the elitist nature of the Costa Rican educational system.

In 1965 less than 1 percent of the entire population had attended a university for one or more years. An examination of civil service roles and job evaluations, on the other hand, and a cursory inspection of positions in private enterprise reveal that a university degree is the key to the top administrative and policy-making positions in the country. Goldrich refers to a very small, highly advantaged educational elite in Costa Rica.[9] A degree also conveys a great amount of status in the social swing of things. Like other republics in North and South America, Costa Rica has abolished the few hereditary titles that existed in the country during the colonial period; however, members of the upper social sectors invariably affix their university degree, whatever the level, to their names. A graduate of a four-year undergraduate course, regardless of subject matter, becomes addressed as *licenciado*. Engineers, architects, lawyers, and professors are addressed by their titles rather than as *señor*. A special office in the Ministry of Education evaluates the degrees obtained at foreign universities and issues an appropriate title.

TENSION MANAGEMENT

The Costa Rican educational apparatus functions as a tension management mechanism for the society with its scarce economic and status resources. For the working class in general, the primary method for climbing into the upper or prestige class is through this educational system. And yet the economy and public administra-

9 Goldrich, *Sons of the Establishment*, p. 17.

tion are certainly not capable of providing jobs for a large group of university graduates annually. Even though the number of government jobs has doubled in the last two decades, there are not enough to compensate for the rapid population growth rates; the demand for white-collar jobs could far outstrip their availability if some control were not exerted on the production of this kind of worker. This is particularly true since other areas of the economic system have not upped their employment capabilities as the data in Table 1 show. The present university system funnels the number of highly trained white-collar workers down to a trickle, assuring status employment for all who graduate. Thus the situation in prerevolutionary Cuba is avoided, where a large group of underemployed and highly trained personnel eventually became sufficiently dissident to alter the system.

However, although the educational system in Costa Rica promotes stability, it hardly could be qualified as promoting upward social mobility for the working class as Solari intimates. One of the questions which will be posed throughout this analysis is whether or not there are not too many of these tension management mechanisms operating in a country which is in need of change if economic development is to occur.

It should be pointed out that through the 1960s at least, the Costa Rican economic system, most particularly the public administration, has supplied jobs to the majority of those leaving high school and incapable of entering the university for one reason or another. It is possible that this group could become a source of tension in the future, but only if employment opportunities became more scarce. Most of the unemployment in Costa Rica occurs among the working classes who leave school after only a few years and who are forced to assume seasonal positions in agriculture or a submarginal city job.

Richard N. Adams has asserted that a bifurcated class structure is typical of most Latin American nations.[10] This is certainly the case in Costa Rica. Within each of the two classes of society, upward social mobility is achieved in a different fashion. For members of the upper class the way to get ahead is through the accumulation of status resources such as joining the right club, receiving

---

[10] R. N. Adams, "Introduction (to Social Organization in Latin America)," in D. B. Heath and R. N. Adams (eds.), *Contemporary Cultures and Societies of Latin America* (New York: Random House, 1965).

invitations to prestigious functions, making the right contacts, and occupying a political role for a period of time. Within the lower class the method for getting ahead is through the accumulation of scarce economic resources; in other words, for a member of the working class to achieve upward social mobility, he must make more money. It is not unusual to find a member of the lower class, a skilled craftsman perhaps, who has no status in Costa Rican society, making more money than certain white-collar workers in the prestige class.

Money and status are not necessarily synonymous in Costa Rica. It is virtually impossible for a member of the working class to accumulate enough status to become accepted in the upper class. However, if he accumulates enough wealth, he may be able to send his children to private high schools and maybe to the university, purchasing for them enough status to go through the barrier to upward social mobility.

The Class Structure

It is not only in the educational system and in patterns of social mobility that evidences of a bifurcated society present themselves. There are symptoms of social elitism throughout Costa Rican society. In a recent study of San José's Central Penitentiary it was discovered that out of 840 prisoners interned at the time, only five could be classed as members of the upper class.[11] Four of the five were office clerks—white-collar workers with only marginal status—and only one could be considered as a person in possession of a considerable amount of status. Needless to say, the status was becoming rapidly depleted during the man's term as a prisoner.

The method by which the Costa Rican government obtains its taxes is further evidence of the class bias of political decision makers. The taxation system clearly works against the individual with less income. Although, with the encouragement of the United States Agency for International Development (AID) and other international agencies, Costa Rica now has an income tax, it is almost negligible, and enforcement is sporadic and uneven. Instead

[11] Iglesia Episcopal, "Encuesta sobre datos en los archivos del consejo Superior de Defensa Social: Penitenciaría Central," July 17–August 23, 1967, mimeo.

the government primarily obtains its revenues from duties levied on imports and from a recently established sales tax which ranges from 5 to 25 percent of the value of certain articles. If only luxury items incurred import duties or were liable to the sales tax, no accusations could be leveled against the system for penalizing the poorer man. However, in 1966 the Costa Rican government obtained nearly $1.3 million in revenues from import duties levied on foodstuffs.

CLASS NORMS

The Costa Rican class structure varies in some respects from the Latin American patterns described above and alluded to by Richard N. Adams. A principal variance is the allegiance to democratic norms which members of the upper social sectors demonstrate. These norms, which have been promoted in the system by the propaganda of the National Liberation Party (PLN) and other organizations, have become thoroughly internalized by the elite. This allegiance to democratic norms is held concomitantly with a second principal trait, which is an incrementalist attitude toward change. Radical changes are mistrusted by this group; and, as problems are faced, the upper class prefers decisions which do not disrupt the present socioeconomic and political systems to any notable degree. Under the leadership of members of the upper class a participant, elaborately checked-and-balanced, governmental structure has been created in Costa Rica, hampering broader-scale, integrated problem solving for the society, a problem which will be examined in succeeding chapters. Also under the leadership of this class the educational system has become a control mechanism, labor unions are frowned upon, and business practices are noncompetitive, attuned to low turnover and maximum profit per-unit-sold type operations. Secularization, the separation of social and political processes from a particular religious belief system, although officially condoned, is severely restricted in practice.

Some of the methods by which members of the upper-status group of the society can rise socially within their own class have been discussed above. These techniques for rising socially have become so institutionalized that Costa Ricans can use some of them simply by outlaying a certain amount of money, assuming the minimum amount of status which permits them to be accepted in the prestige class. For example, San José's leading newspaper, *La Nación*, with a circulation of sixty thousand, devotes about one-third of its space to its social section. The paper, which in the period beginning October 1, 1967, and ending February 28, 1968, ran a picture of Pope Paul VI on its front page fifty times, receives sizeable revenues from paid announcements about births, debuts, engagements, and teas and cocktails pertaining to the prestige class of the society. The social climber regards getting his name in the paper as a key method for obtaining status, even if it does cost him money. Prestigious social functions have become so institutionalized that simply by paying an initiation fee the social climber with a minimum amount of status can hobnob at certain events with members of higher society, including political decision makers who are regarded as possessing great status. The weekly Diplomats and Foreigners Tea is a good example of this type of function. For only $4.50 yearly, the women of the upper social sector can meet with others of their kind—ambassadors' wives, government officials, and so forth—each Monday to sew or to play bridge.

Conspicuous consumption is still another method for climbing ahead. Marginal members of the prestige class, occupiers of clerical positions for example, will spend relatively great sums of money on their clothing. When entertaining they serve only Scotch whisky, which retails eleven dollars for a fifth of a gallon, rather than spirits manufactured locally. Every effort is made by this group to purchase as many imported articles and commodities as possible, since this is still another way of achieving status. The general attitude of the upper class is that only poor people purchase locally manufactured products. The effects that this posture on their part has had on Costa Rica's balance-of-payment situation is discussed in the next chapter.

THE WORKING CLASS

The outlook of members of the rural-dwelling working class, which constitutes the majority of the lower social sector in Costa Rica, is formed at least in part by the patterns of land tenure. The pattern which land tenure has taken, the fact that so many do own land even if their holding is not farmable economically, has often been hailed as a prime cause for the existence of "democratic government" in the country. As Goldrich states:

A factor that has been considered by many to be the basis of Costa Rica's relatively democratic history is the wide distribution of land ownership, the relatively large proportion of small and medium farm properties.[12]

As will be discussed, it is this very "democracy," so favored by the prestige class, which at times has impeded coherent reform and badly needed change in the country. If land tenure patterns are principal bulwarks of the present "democratic" institutional pattern, then they are impeding not only economic and agricultural development but also effective problem solving for the society as a whole. José Abdulio Cordero provides a less idealistic and probably more accurate picture of the small landholder whom he describes as

wrapped up in his small inherited land holding, fearful of the new, abjected, peaceful, completely against taxes, indifferent to politics and religious but not saintly.[13]

The small landholder, or *minifundista*, often has to seek employment on neighboring large farms in order to obtain cash for certain necessary purchases. Besides the economic implications of having to seek employment, there is a major social and political consequence for the *minifundista*. For he is anything but the independent individual he is believed to be in some quarters, and he undoubtedly learns submissive authoritarian postures toward the upper class early in his life. It is improbable that this submissiveness leads the *minifundista* to a position of apathy as in some other Latin American countries, but it certainly affects such things as his voting behavior and his participation in decision making. It is probable—and there is no empirical information available about this—that the larger landowner is the opinion leader of his neighborhood.

As will be seen in the succeeding chapter, the economic situation of the urban lower class is not a good one. The ever-swelling group of urban poor, attracted to the cities not by industrial jobs but generally by the more advanced social infrastructure to be found in these areas, in many ways is living at a standard lower than the one of the rural working class. It is not unusual, for example, for

[12] Goldrich, *Sons of the Establishment*, p. 27.

[13] José Abdulio Cordero, *El ser de la nacionalidad Costarricense* (Madrid: Editorial Tridente, S.A. 1964), p. 33.

members of this group to be forced to erect their own dwellings because of a shortage of slum housing. The flimsy shacks and wooden hovels in which they are forced to live are scattered throughout principal urban areas. The crowded conditions and the filth in which many of these people live undoubtedly have profound effects on their social and political outlooks. However, while the rural poor may have no hope of ever becoming the equal of the wealthier landlords, the urban working-class member can expect, because of the availability of schools, at least to see his children get ahead. Upward social mobility, although extremely difficult in any case, is more facile for the urban poor simply because there are more opportunities for them in the cities.

The urban working class is the most anomic of all social sectors in Costa Rica. Ties having been broken with their rural past, new friends and new kinship relationships often must be established. These disruptions are coupled with a sense of rising expectations, particularly of the economic variety. Deprived of effective status leadership, the urban poor have not counted much in the political arena. Since this group grows at a rate of only .6 percent faster than the population as a whole, it is not gaining strength by virtue of numbers in any significant sense. Costa Rica is still essentially a rural, agrarian society, and the country's major party, the PLN, has still been able to win elections by receiving the support of the rural, not the urban, areas. As the urban poor become more capable of swinging elections in one direction or another and of making more powerful demands, their participation in the society will probably become more important.

Although class lines are less pronounced in Costa Rica than in other Latin American countries, they are there nevertheless and clearly recognized by the population. In his study of the attitudes prevalent among upper-class high school students, Goldrich found that 60 percent of those interviewed agreed that "social class distinctions are inevitable," while 25 percent believed that "family position or money" were "most important for success in this country."[14] Upward social mobility, while perhaps easier in Costa Rica than in some other nations of Latin America, is certainly not unconstrained. With a fast-growing population, a more slowly developing educational system, a regressive taxation system, and a *mini-*

fundio land tenure pattern, mobility is not easy. The norms held by the upper, or "prestige," class, democratic in tone but elitist in practice, seem to be one contributing impediment to enhanced opportunities for the lower class. The authoritarian and submissive attitudes of the rural working population coupled with an anomic, albeit nonapathetic, attitude on the part of the urban poor are the second principal impediments to upward social mobility.

Social Integration

Costa Rica does not suffer from the severe racial, linguistic, and geographic differences so characteristic of several other of the Latin American nations. Less than one-half of 1 percent of the total population can be characterized as indigenous, wearing native costumes and speaking a non-Spanish language. These people live in tiny isolated communities near the southern or northern borders of Panama or Nicaragua. About 2 percent of the population is Negro, and in the past there has been some evidence of racial discrimination against this group. Brought to Costa Rica from the British West Indies to build a railroad or to work on banana plantations, most of the Negroes live along the Atlantic coast and speak an English dialect.

In the past Negroes were not permitted to move into the central plateau through a series of extralegal measures aimed against them. This restriction and the depression of the 1930s led many of these descendants of West Indians to emigrate to the Panama Canal Zone. However, this discrimination has now been terminated, although it is still difficult for a Negro to get a job in the central plateau. It is safe to predict that in the long run this group will be assimilated.

More than 97 percent of Costa Ricans are either Caucasians of Spanish or Italian descent or mestizos (Spanish-Indian mixture), and the entire population speaks the Spanish language. Racial, linguistic, and regional factors are not importantly affecting the integration of Costa Rica, nor do they adversely affect either vertical or horizontal social mobility. Costa Rica is an essentially integrated country.

2
The Economic Environment

The ability of a society to transform itself is always directly dependent on the extent of resources of all types available to it. Some resources can easily be imported. But usually change depends on having certain basic resources—natural, technological, economic, and human—actually available within a country. Its name notwithstanding, Costa Rica does not possess a "rich coast." Nor can the mountainous interior of the tiny nation, where a majority of the population live, be labeled anything but positively poor.

The economy of Costa Rica essentially is dependent on its agricultural resources. Products of the soil, particularly bananas and coffee, constitute the country's principal exports. Almost one-half of the entire work force devotes itself to growing crops for itself, for the other half of the population, and for international markets. Although efforts are being made by decision makers to diversify the economy and its exports, to introduce industry, and to strengthen the service sector, it is safe to predict that Costa Rica will have to grow cash crops for the international market for many years.

Realizing that the cultivation and sale of cash crops for the international market provide foreign exchange badly needed, not only to finance the industrialization effort but also to finance the purchase of commodities which are unavailable in the country, Costa Ricans have placed as much of their farmland into this type of endeavor as possible. Although in the latter part of the twentieth century other export crops, notably coffee, have challenged the banana for supremacy, this fruit continues to play an exceedingly important role in the economic system. Unfortunately a side effect of the effort to grow cash crops for export has been neglect of the cultivation of staple commodities needed for consumption within the country. A result of this situation is the curious spectacle of an agrarian economy unable to feed itself. This chapter contains a brief introduction to the economic system of Costa Rica, its problems, and how these problems relate to other sectors of the society.

The Agricultural Sector

One indication of the importance of a particular sector of an economy is the percentage of the national work force which it employs. As can be seen in Table 1, although the percentage of the

Table 1
EMPLOYMENT BY SECTORS OF ECONOMY IN CENSUS YEARS
(percentages of working force)

Employed in	1927	1950	1963
Industry	8%	11%	12%
Agriculture and fishing	62	55	49
Government	—	5	10
Commerce	6	8	7
Service	14[a]	15	17
Other	10	6	5
Total	100%	100%	100%

SOURCE: Dirección General de Estadística y Censo, Censo de población, 1950 and Censo de población, 1963.

[a] Includes government.

Costa Rican population employed in agricultural pursuits is diminishing, this sector is still the largest job provider. And yet this large group of workers does not contribute to the gross national product in proportion to its numbers. While almost half of the entire working population is employed in agriculture, this sector produces only 30 percent of the gross national product as shown in Table 2.

A principal factor contributing to the low productive level of Costa Rican agriculturalists is the pattern of land tenure to be

Table 2
MAKEUP AND GROWTH RATE BY SECTOR
OF COSTA RICAN GROSS NATIONAL PRODUCT
(in percentages)

A. Makeup

Sector	1950	1955	1960	1963	1966
Agriculture	41%	35%	31%	29%	29%
Industry (manufacturing)	12	13	14	15	16
Commerce	14	15	14	14	14
Service	14	14	14	15	15
Government	5	8	9	10	9
Other (transportation, energy, housing)	14	15	18	17	17
TOTAL (G.N.P.)	100%	100%	100%	100%	100%

B. Average Annual Growth Rates by Sector

Sector	1950–1955	1955–1960	1960–1966	1950–1966
Gross National Product	8.4%	6.5%	5.5%	6.6%
Agricultural Sector	6.3	3.8	6.8	5.7
Construction	18.7	3.2	6.9	9.2
Industry (manufacturing)	12.3	7.9	10.4	10.2
Government	18.5	11.6	8.3	11.3
Commerce	10.4	6.6	7.2	8.0
Service	10.1	7.7	8.7	8.8
Other (transportation, energy, housing)	10.6	8.5	8.3	9.1

SOURCE: Presidencia de la República, Oficina de Planificación, *Compendio de cifras básicas de Costa Rica* (San José, 1967), p. 4; Oficina de Planificación, *La economía de Costa Rica en 1966*, p. 8.

found in the countryside. Although the situation is not so acute as in some of the other Latin American nations, this particular country is characterized by a large number of very small landowners who contribute little or nothing to the national economy and who perform agricultural labor on a full-time basis. In 1963 there were a total of 64,721 farms in Costa Rica, 76 percent of which were cultivated by the owner of the property himself.[1] However, 27,925, or 43 percent of these farms, were under seventeen acres in size

[1] Dirección General de Estadística y Censo, *Censo agropecuario, 1963* (San José, November, 1965), p. 17.

and, as a result, too small to be economically viable.[2] On these small farms, or *minifundia* as they are sometimes known, the owners are growing just enough staple foodstuffs for their families' needs and in many cases are accepting seasonal employment, if available, on neighboring larger farms to obtain cash for certain types of purchases at the local market.

There are several results of this situation. First, the land on the *minifundio* is not being used to its best potential. Mechanization is not possible, and nothing is being raised to feed the nonagricultural portion of the population. Since larger farms are oriented towards producing cash crops for export, there is a perpetual shortage of staple foodstuffs in the country. Food prices for industrial and government workers and for the urban poor are relatively high because of a limited supply. In order to alleviate the situation, food is often imported. In 1965, for example, Costa Rica imported $14 million worth of foodstuffs that included over $1 million worth of rice and beans, the principal staples in the diets of all Costa Ricans.[3] In 1966 food imports climbed in value to almost $16 million, this figure including $2 million worth of rice and beans.[4] For a country which places half of its laboring force into growing crops and raising livestock and which exports primarily agricultural products to have to import foodstuffs means that there is clearly a need for some change in the basic orientation of the farmers.

Looking for a moment at the large farms, in 1963 there were only fifty-nine in Costa Rica containing more than 5,970 acres; but the total area of these threescore operations was almost double that of the 43,199 farms containing less than fifty acres.[5] It is interesting to note that of the large farms, only three of the owners resided on and managed their own properties. Side by side with the *minifundio*,

---

[2] The Costa Rican Institute of Land and Colonization (ITCO) has stated in a recent study that as far as that country is concerned independent farms under seventeen acres in size are not viable. ITCO, "Tenencia y uso de la tierra en Costa Rica," unpublished mimeo, p. 28. Needless to say, the size of a minimally landed farm for a viable operation depends on many variables including soil, altitude, and rainfall patterns.

[3] Dirección General de Estadística y Censo, *Comercio Exterior de Costa Rica, 1965* (San José, 1966), p. 1.

[4] Dirección General de Estadística y Censo, *Comercio Exterior de Costa Rica, 1966* (San José, 1967), p. 1.

[5] Dirección General de Estadística y Censo, *Censo Agropecuario, 1963*, p. 17.

then, there is also some degree of absentee *latifundismo*, a term sometimes used to label large, very inefficient agricultural operations. However, the picture is not wholly a bleak one, particularly if compared with some of Costa Rica's neighbors. Some 20,540 farms, or 32 percent of the total number of agricultural operations in the country, are medium in size, feasible to operate economically, and managed by their owners. However, this is not to suggest that there is a kind of middle-class farmer in Costa Rica. The owners of the medium-sized operations, like their very large neighbors, are principally interested in growing cash crops—coffee in the mountains or bananas in the coastal regions. They usually do no manual labor themselves, but rather hire their neighboring *minifundista* to do all of the work for them.

For many years the owners of the larger farms fought all efforts made by the government to have them diversify away from the cultivation of only two commodities for export. Although they have not diversified to the extent of growing staple foodstuffs to sell on the local market, they have begun to produce a variety of export crops. In the long run, at least, this will help to limit Costa Rica's helplessness in the face of the vagaries of the international commodity markets. As can be noted in Table 3, bananas and coffee,

Table 3

COMPOSITION OF COSTA RICAN EXPORTS IN PERCENTAGES
(based on 1962 U.S. dollars)

	Coffee	Bananas	Cacao	Sugar	Beef	Others[a]	Total[b]
1950	31.3%	60.5%	3.3%	.1%	—	—	95.2%
1960	45.0	28.7	5.2	2.7	6.0	12.4	100.0
1965	37.0	26.0	2.4	4.4	3.1	27.6	100.0

SOURCE: Presidencia de la República, Oficina de Planificación, *Compendio de cifras basicas: Comercio exterior 1950–1965* (San José, 1967).

[a] This figure includes manufactured products, which have increased considerably since Costa Rica joined the Central American Common Market.

[b] Percentages do not total out in 1950 because of the inexactness of statistics.

which in 1950 constituted 90 percent of all exports, now make up only 60 percent of the total.

The diversification has not increased the demand for agricultural labor to any great extent because none of the cash crops are of the type which are labor-intensive. During relatively brief harvest seasons, workers are recruited; but employment in any one area of the country rarely lasts for over three months. In the case of the banana workers, who are organized, some provision is usually made for the welfare of labor in the nonharvest seasons.

In the final analysis the Costa Rican agricultural sector is not meeting the country's needs. Productivity must be improved drastically and diversification must occur more rapidly if the country's total number of resources for change are to be increased. One proposed solution to the problem is a change in the pattern of land tenure in the country, a change which can be carried out only through the political arena. Since the very basis of economic position and, indirectly, political power in Costa Rica rests on the ownership of land, changes in this area could cause disruptions affecting the entire social fabric of the country.

The Governmental Sector

The government of Costa Rica has become increasingly involved in the economy in recent years, not only as a consumer but also as a producer and investor. As shown in Table 1, between 1950 and 1966 the government doubled the percentage of the national work force which it employs. This is a rate of growth unmatched by any other sector of the economy. During the same sixteen-year period the government, through its various institutions, raised the percentage it consumed of the national income from 9 to nearly 15 percent. The government's contribution to the gross national product and the growth of this sector in comparison to others of the economy are revealed in Table 2. Also since 1955 the government has accounted for at least 20 percent of total annual capital investment.[6] The government has been capable of carrying out these activities by continuously engaging in deficit spending. Between 1955 and 1958, for example, while revenues grew at the lower rate of 3.7 percent annually, expenses rose at an average annual rate of 11.9 percent.[7] A considerable portion of the deficit was covered by borrowing abroad, still another factor underlying

[6] Dirección General de Estadística y Censo, *La Economía de Costa Rica en 1966*, p. 27.

[7] Ibid., p. 28.

Costa Rica's dependence on the external environment. As a result of these governmental deficits and the fact that the agricultural sector has been incapable of producing enough cash crops to meet the demand for foreign exchange, devaluation of the currency has also been necessary.

The government is a producer and owner not only of public services and utilities such as highways, hospitals, schools, and electric power facilities but also of consumer goods and services and industrial and commercial facilities. A government monopoly manufactures all alcoholic beverages produced in the country with the exception of beer. Government monopolies also own and operate a railway from the capital city of San José to the Pacific Ocean, the national banking system, the country's only insurance company, and its only petroleum refinery; the government is the principal shareholder of LACSA international airlines. One government institution not only finances the construction of housing for the poor, but also provides tools and materials, and in some cases builds the edifice. Approximately 10 percent of all persons over twelve years of age in 1963 were employed by the government, its agencies, or semiautonomous institutions.

The government has even begun since the early 1960s to intervene in the agricultural sector. Although the principal reason for the establishment of the *Instituto Nacional de Tierras y Colonizaje* (ITCO), the national agrarian institute, was to correct the land-tenure situation already described by establishing peasants on viable plots of land, this agency has also assumed the responsibilities for marketing the produce of its colonies. To date, the redistribution program has progressed at a snail's pace, but one colony, a former United Fruit Company plantation, has already begun to produce notable quantities of bananas for export.

The Private Sector

Although the industrial portion of the private sector of the Costa Rican economy has been growing in terms of output in recent years, as can be seen in Tables 1 and 2, it is only of secondary importance as a provider of employment in a country with one of the fastest-growing populations in the world. The private sector has not even kept pace with the government as a new job provider.

Between 1960 and 1966, although government payrolls swelled faster than did those of the private sector, the latter's contribution from industry to the gross national product grew faster than did the contribution from government. Commerce, both retail and wholesale, which had until recently contributed more to the gross national product than had any other group in the private sector, did not grow at the same rate as did manufacturing in this period.

Up until Costa Rica joined the Central American Common Market (CACM) in 1963, industry had been heavily overprotected from international competitors, a factor which led to the establishment there of many at best marginal manufacturing plants. Although the country remains highly protectionist in terms of its general tariff structure, membership in the CACM has meant that most industries now receive little or no protection from competition originating in other nations of the Central American isthmus. CACM membership has brought some competition and a brisk expansion in the market available to Costa Rican manufacturers, insuring a certain degree of modernization in both business attitudes and in the way plants are organized and operated. Retail and wholesale businessmen have not benefited similarly from the CACM membership. In general, members of this group retain traditional attitudes toward competition, service, investments, and new products. Costa Rican wholesalers and retailers seek the maximum profit on each item sold, rather than attempt to obtain a high rate of turnover at a lower profit per item. The principles of volume selling are unknown. Fixed prices, however, have begun to prevail with the exception of public open markets and ventures devoted to selling souvenirs to tourists. Since the North American tourist has now come to believe that bargaining is expected of him, prices are adjusted accordingly.

A great deal of wholesale and retail business efforts are devoted to the promotion and sale of imported commodities. Demand for this type of commodity, particularly among the upper social sectors, is already high; and the promotional efforts of businessmen has increased it even further. In the absence of a concerted "buy Costa Rican" campaign, a great deal of foreign exchange is being used to finance the purchase of these imported articles by better-off members of the populace. A seemingly unbreakable system is thus established with the upper social sectors consuming large amounts of foreign exchange in purchasing their commodity imports, necessitating increases in the yield of cash crops for export. However, these increases are used to purchase food imports, required because too much land is being cultivated in bananas, coffee, and sugar; as a result, the country cannot feed itself. The government, which engages in deficit spending, uses foreign exchange to make up its unbalanced budget. The effect of this system is to leave very little foreign exchange for financing industrialization, for importing capital equipment, or even for purchasing farm equipment. This requires further borrowing abroad, the commitment of even larger cash crops in the future to meet payments, and the probability that the Costa Rican poor will pay higher prices for their rice and beans in the future.

The Money Economy

The money economy of Costa Rica, just as in any country with a per capita income of approximately four hundred dollars, is very limited.[8] As a result, only a limited number of items can be produced for consumption solely within the country on an economical basis, and industrialization efforts are severely hampered. Unfortunately, for many years public and private industrialization efforts were oriented almost exclusively toward producing for the tiny national market, hardly a profitable or economically feasible orientation. With the advent of the Central American Common Market, the newer industries now locating within Costa Rica have been geared toward producing for export and have not been as limited in their market potential or as hampered by high per-unit costs.

In considering a money economy it is enlightening to view income distribution figures, which in a very limited sense are provided in Table 4. Insight derived from these figures is limited for several reasons. First, the figures are drawn exclusively from the San José area. Second, they are rather old. Unfortunately, surveys of this nature are not taken with any regularity, and these are the most recent figures available. In any case, since 1961, although absolute income figures as a whole have undoubtedly risen, it

---

[8] Various Costa Rican sources differ on the per capita income of the country. Based on a 1966 G.N.P. of $622 million, per capita income is $425.

Table 4
SAN JOSÉ INCOME DISTRIBUTION
(1961)

Monthly Family Income (U.S. Dollars)	Percentage of Families
From 0 to 22	41.6%
From 22 to 45	31.9
From 45 to 67	11.6
From 67 to 90	5.7
From 90 to 112	3.7
From 112 to 135	3.1
Over 135	2.4
Total	100.0%

SOURCE: Oficina de Planificación, *Características de la economía de Costa Rica, 1950–1962*, p. 351.

would seem doubtful that the percentages have shown much change. The data also provide some orientation toward the class structure of the country.

Coupled with the extremely inequitable distribution of income in Costa Rica is an employment problem of major proportions. Because of an extremely rapid population growth rate it is necessary for the economy to provide jobs for fifteen thousand new workers every year.[9] The official unemployment rate is 7 percent, and much of it is comprised of new workers seeking a job for the first time.[10] It is probable that if persons who are only seasonally employed in agriculture and the *minifundistas* are considered to be technically unemployed, the percentage of Costa Rica's work force without a job would be much larger than revealed from official statistics.

Of particular importance when regarding Costa Rican employment statistics and income sources and particularly relevant to the study of national politics is the fact that in 1963, for example, 30 percent of all white-collar positions were filled in the public administration, its agencies, and semiautonomous institutions.[11] Many of the white-collar workers hold down more than one posi-

[9] Oficina de Planificación, *Características de la economía de Costa Rica, 1950–1962*, p. 329.

[10] *La economía de Costa Rica en 1966*, p. 38.

[11] *Censo de población, 1963*, p. 297.

tion, and it would appear safe to estimate that a minimum 50 percent of all upper social sector workers in Costa Rica rely at least in part on the government for their income.

External Factors

The reliance of the economy of Costa Rica on a few exports and its direct dependence on external factors has briefly been alluded to above. The effects of this external influence can be seen and felt not only in the economy itself, but also indirectly in other spheres of the society. Table 5 shows the gross national product,

Table 5
COSTA RICA'S IMPORTS AND EXPORTS IN RELATION TO GROSS
NATIONAL PRODUCT (G.N.P.)
(millions of 1962 U.S. dollars)

	G.N.P.	Imports	Exports	Imports as Percent of G.N.P.	Exports as Percent of G.N.P.	Balance of Trade
1950	222.7	74.6	56.7	33.4	25.5	—17.9
1955	333.1	104.6	74.4	31.5	22.5	—30.2
1960	451.7	127.7	104.1	28.2	22.7	—23.6
1966	622.1	206.9	155.9	33.3	25.1	—51.0

SOURCE: Oficina de Planificación, *La economía de Costa Rica en 1966*, p. 18.

the country's exports and imports converted to dollars, and the percentages of the gross national product which are made up from foreign trade. This table not only gives some indication of the heavy reliance of the national economy on external factors, but also reveals the growing deficit incurred because of the trade imbalance.

A nation heavily dependent on selling a few agricultural commodities to keep its economy stable might do well to seek out several customers for its products. This might enable it to avoid a subordinate relationship with a single customer and possibly even indirect political influence over its decision-making process. As the figures in Table 6 show, the international economic situation of Costa Rica is quite different from the ideal. By far the largest purchaser of the Central America nation's exports is the United

Table 6

TOTAL UNITED STATES IMPORTATION OF PRINCIPAL
COSTA RICAN EXPORTS

(millions of U.S. dollars at current exchange rates)

	1964	1965	1966
Total Costa Rican banana exports	$28.3	$28.3	$29.1
U.S. Imports of Costa Rican bananas	28.2	26.0	27.5
Percent of Costa Rican bananas imported by U.S.	99%	91%	94%
Total Costa Rican coffee exports	$48.0	$46.6	$52.6
U.S. Imports of Costa Rican coffee	15.0	18.0	13.5
Percent of Costa Rican coffee imported by U.S.	31%	38%	26%
Total Costa Rican cacao exports	$4.0	$2.0	$3.1
U.S. Imports of Costa Rican cacao	2.9	1.4	1.8
Percent of Costa Rican cacao imported by U.S.	73%	64%	58%

SOURCE: Ministerio de Industria y Comercio, *Comercio exterior de Costa Rica, 1965*, pp. xx–xxi, and *Comercio exterior de Costa Rica, 1966*, pp. xxi–xxii.

States. Since principal exports are foods, Costa Rica's economic well-being is dependent to a certain extent on the whim of the North American housewife who primarily purchases these kinds of products. In the case of bananas, where a single United States firm, the United Fruit Company and its subsidiary, the Standard Fruit Company, have been the principal producers and exporters for many years, it is hardly unexpected that many Costa Ricans think this firm capable of exerting considerable pressure on national decision makers.

The balance of payments situation faced by Costa Rica is more complicated than would appear from the data in Table 5; for the tiny nation has managed to pay for its large quantity of imports annually by luring larger amounts of public and private capital into the country. Unfortunately, the long-run effect has been to put the country into such a position of external debt that each year a sizeable portion of dollars and other foreign currencies earned by exports are used for payment of interest on borrowed capital, for amortization of debts, and for profits which are exported to the lender nation or nations. Interest payments on borrowed capital alone have grown from $13 million in 1950 to $18 million in 1966, an increase of 38 percent.[12]

[12] *La economía de Costa Rica en 1966*, pp. 26–42.

One of the brighter spots in the external relationships of the Costa Rican economy is the Central American Common Market (CACM). Although Costa Rica did not join the regional association until September, 1963, five years after the founding of the CACM, it has broadened the economic future of the former. Table 7 pro-

Table 7
GROWTH OF COSTA RICAN-CENTRAL AMERICAN TRADE

Year	Exports to Central America (millions of dollars)	Percent Increase over Previous Year	Imports from Central America (millions of dollars)	Percent Increase over Previous Year
1960	$2.4	—	$3.5	—
1961	2.2	—8	4.0	14
1962	1.9	—14	3.3	—18
1963	4.3	113	3.9	18
1964	10.5	114	8.4	115
1965	18.2	73	14.7	75

SOURCES: CEPAL, *Evaluación de la integración económica en Centro-America*, pp. 258-259, and *Comercio exterior de Costa Rica, 1965*, p. xii.

vides data demonstrating the effects that CACM membership has had on Costa Rica's trade with its four neighbors to the north— Nicaragua, Honduras, El Salvador, and Guatemala.

In addition to increasing intraregional trade in Central America, the CACM has helped to further industrial expansion within the five countries. For one thing the agreement has brought competition to long-sheltered and inefficient operations. But more important are the effects of Article 17 of the General Treaty of Central American Economic Integration, which provides for a program of integrated industries.[13] Realizing that the money economy of all five members of the CACM is just barely capable of efficiently supporting certain larger industries, Article 17 limits the number of this type of operation permitted to locate on the isthmus. Thus the integrated industries program is an agreement that the area as a whole will be limited to one or two manufacturers of a certain

[13] Joseph Pincus, *El Mercado Común Centroamericano* (Mexico, D.F.: ROCAP, 1963), p. 76.

product—such as automobile tires, which require a sizeable investment and a larger volume of sales than can be provided within any single Central American nation. Costa Rica already has two of these industries in operation within its borders—a fertilizer plant in the Pacific port city of Puntarenas and an automobile tire plant located on the outskirts of the capital city of San José.

Analysts of the CACM assert that one of the principal factors contributing to the preliminary success of this regional association is the fact that it is essentially nonpolitical by nature.[14] For example, for some time Costa Rica refused to recognize diplomatically the military governments which came to power in Guatemala and Honduras in 1963. But because economic integration is an issue that arouses little emotion, Costa Rica participated in all CACM meetings with representatives of the very governments that it refused to recognize.[15]

In the late 1960s the CACM received a blow which could limit its usefulness or even bring the association to dissolution. The first war between two American states since the 1930s involved two of the CACM members—El Salvador and Honduras. The so-called "soccer war" has cut the CACM in half and made overland transportation of goods between Guatemala on the one hand and Costa Rica and Nicaragua on the other hand at times impossible. It will take many years for the area to return to normalcy.

Summary

Costa Rica, an independent republic, has a population smaller than the city of Miami and a buying power and economic resources which are only a fraction of this single United States city. The Central American republic depends on agriculture as the mainstay of its economy, importing more than it exports, and producing a limited variety of cash crops to pay for its imports. By devoting a large portion of its efforts to the growing of these cash crops for export, the intense cultivation of staple foodstuffs needed to supply a rapidly growing population is often neglected; and, as a result,

[14] Joseph S. Nye, Jr., "Central American Regional Integration," *International Conciliation*, No. 572 (March, 1967), 20–22.

[15] Ibid., p. 28.

the country imports such staples as rice, beans, and corn in varying quantities almost annually.

The government has become increasingly involved in the economic system since 1948 as a producer, a consumer, and most importantly as a purveyor of jobs. The industrial contribution to the private sector of the economy has been growing in terms of the percentage which it contributes to the gross national product, but not in terms of the number of jobs which it provides. This industrial growth has at least partially been the result of the impetus originating with the economic integration of the Central American isthmus. Whether or not the CACM will encourage the establishment of large-scale industries in the five countries and a resultant diminishment in their dependence on agriculture and the world market remains to be seen.

At the close of the 1960s the picture was not a bright one, particularly when war erupted between two of the members of the CACM—Honduras and El Salvador. And even despite this war, considering that the money economies of Costa Rica and its four neighbors are very poor, it would appear that large-scale industrialization can be little more than a very long-run project. The development of agricultural productivity must be the keynote to the Costa Rican economy for many years to come.

3
Political Institutions

The authentic Latin American revolutionary must maintain an unshakable respect for personal liberties while fighting to transform the existing structures of our countries. . . In my opinion when a revolution ceases to respect personal liberties it ceases to be a revolution and becomes a regression.[1]

The Antecedents

As is true of any political institutions, their antecedents have had profound effects on the form which they take at any particular point in time. In order to provide some perspective on the historical influences on Costa Rica's political institutions, an extremely brief and sketchy résumé of its political history beginning in 1940 is presented below.

THE PREREVOLUTIONARY PERIOD

The modern period of Costa Rican history begins in 1940, for it is at that date that personalities still very much in the public eye came to the foreground and when battlelines of modern political history were drawn for the country. In 1940 medical doctor Rafael Calderón Guardia, an immensely popular individual, was elected to the presidency. Calderón and his followers, known as *calderonistas,* reestablished the long defunct National University; negotiated a long-standing dispute with Panama over the boundaries between

[1] Luis Alberto Monge, *No hay revolución sin libertad* (San José, 1961), p. 8.

the two countries; and, with the help and support of the president's personal National Republican Party (PRN), put Costa Rica's first labor code into law. As a result of the new legislation, the only labor union then in existence, later to be known as *Vanguardia Popular*, which was communist-organized and operated, was finally permitted to function legally. The union quickly gained considerable strength, particularly in the North American-owned banana plantations, where organizing efforts and strikes had been occurring for almost a decade.

Calderón Guardia was not a very practical administrator despite his achievements, and it is even rumored that during his term in office, 1940–44, he continued to make house calls and to deliver babies. Because of confusion in the public administration and his prolabor policies, Calderón lost the support of white-collar and many elite groups of the population prior to leaving office. By 1942 the president and his party had to rely more heavily on their *Vanguardia Popular* supporters led by Manuel Mora Valverde, an outspoken San José lawyer.

Constitutionally prohibited from succeeding himself, Calderón arranged for the election of another San José lawyer friend, Teodoro Picado, who assumed the office of chief executive in 1944. During the campaign of that year, Picado was opposed by two groups, one of which was headed by José (popularly known as "Pepe") Figueres Ferrer and the other by Otílio Ulate Blanco. Figueres represented the interests of small rural groups and, to a certain extent, the lower sectors of the prestige class, while Ulate was supported by the old-line elite of his country. Both Figueres and Ulate campaigned against the PRN's reform legislation, social security, and legalized unions. In 1947 the Picado government, which had to rely on *Vanguardia Popular* support even more than had its predecessor, announced that its official candidate for the upcoming 1948 election would be none other than Dr. Rafael Calderón Guardia.

In the face of this announcement and the chaotic financial situation in the republic, a so-called general strike took place in late July, 1947. This strike did not include unions or a significant number of members of the working class, but rather involved the closing of all retail trade establishments, banks, markets, and shops. Picado, after attempting to deal with the strike peacefully for a week, endeavored to use force to reopen trade in the country. The shops of known *calderonista* opponents were systematically looted and many were arrested. This use of force served to alienate the president's opponents further, and the situation rapidly reached a near-crisis level. However, serious violence was averted when on August 1 a group of feminists marched on the presidential palace and the president agreed to listen to their pleas for peace.

In the 1948 election Calderón was opposed by Otílio Ulate, who had the support of Figueres and his followers. When it became apparent that Ulate had won by a small margin—most of the population did not vote at all—the *calderonistas,* who still controlled a majority of the seats in the National Assembly, attempted to nullify the results and declare Calderón the winner. Ulate was imprisoned.

THE 1948 REVOLUTION

Violent opposition broke out against Calderón and his followers in San Isidro el General, some forty-five miles south of the capital city along the Pan American Highway. Led by "Pepe" Figueres, who organized what he called the National Liberation Movement with headquarters at his farm, the opposition forces managed to drive back the first government forces sent against them and then rapidly to gain control of key urban centers surrounding the capital city. According to one historian, when Picado was informed that American military forces from the Panama Canal Zone were about to be sent into the country to "restore peace" and in the face of his defeats in the countryside, he agreed to surrender.[2] However, Manuel Mora, leader of the *Vanguardia Popular,* refused to abide by the Picado-Figueres surrender agreement and a reign of terror settled over San José. The communist union leader retained control of all military installations in the capital city. The Figueres forces made it into San José, and soon fighting was taking place in the city streets themselves. Mora finally surrendered and a junta, headed by Figueres, by then a popular hero, took over the government of the country.

On December 4, 1948, in an unprecedented action in Latin America, Figueres disbanded the military forces of his country. Keys to the main military barracks of San José, the scene of heavy fighting and much bloodshed during the violence of revolution,

---

[2] Ricardo Fernandez Guardia, *Cartilla histórica de Costa Rica* (San José: Imprenta Antonio Lehmann, 1967), p. 162.

were turned over to the minister of education for the purpose of creating a national museum. At about the same time a new loan was negotiated with the United States, and a constituent assembly was elected to write Costa Rica's sixth constitutional document. One of the first actions of the new assembly, in which the followers of Calderón had no representation, was to approve the election of Otílio Ulate in the 1948 election. Figueres was determined to permit Ulate to serve a full term in office before moving directly into the limelight himself. The new constitution, finally written and approved, was ratified on November 7, 1949. Ulate took office as president of Costa Rica the following day.

During the time that the Figueres junta ran Costa Rica, the precedents for many future *liberacionista* actions and policies were set. The junta, for example, created the first two of the many semiautonomous institutions of the public administration now in existence. One of the institutions is made up of the country's entire banking system. Figueres, convinced that the foreign ownership of Costa Rica's banks was detrimental to bringing reform to the country, nationalized and expropriated them all.

THE POSTREVOLUTIONARY PERIOD

Ulate's term-in-office was notoriously uncolorful; and, as the 1953 election drew closer, it became clear that "Pepe" Figueres would be the next chief executive of his country. On October 12, 1951, Figueres had founded the *Partido Liberación Nacional* (PLN) out of the National Liberation Movement which had fought successfully against the *calderonistas* three years earlier. In the 1953 campaign the PLN was the only party to present a comprehensive program to the voter, a pattern which has been repeated in succeeding elections through the late 1960s. Figueres received 65 percent of the presidential vote in the 1953 election and his party an equal percentage of the legislative vote, something which no party, including the PLN, has managed to accomplish since then.

Figueres has always believed that the best method for promoting industrialization in his country is to establish high tariffs.[3] His theory is that high import duties encourage industries to locate within the tariff walls in order to avoid the customs taxes and still

[3] José Figueres, *Cartas a un ciudadano* (San José: Imprenta Nacional, 1956), p. 94.

to sell the market within. In a predominantly agricultural country such as Costa Rica, heavily dependent on imports, the results of large customs duty increases are various and unpredictable. One result, unforeseen by Figueres but noticed by the voters, was a rise in consumer prices.

The PLN leader also believes that, in the case of economically underdeveloped countries, the government must be the principal solver of problems for the society as a whole.[4] Consequently Figueres rapidly involved the government in spheres in which it had not participated prior to 1953; it is for this reason that Table 1—to cite one example of the *liberacionista* program—shows a brisk increase in the employment figures for government after 1950.

As Figueres carried out his program with the help of his political party, he was also building the PLN into a powerful, nationally organized political structure, the first of its kind in the country. This structure has permitted the party to dominate politics in Costa Rica since its inception. The PLN has not lost control of the National Assembly since 1953, although a coalition of the opposition PRN and of Ulate's followers, the *ulatistas*—enemies to the death in 1948—has managed to capture the presidency twice. In fact, since 1953 politics have revolved around the PLN revolutionary program. Rarely is the name *calderonista* or *ulatista* heard in the early 1970s. Today almost everyone is either a *liberacionista* or an *anti-liberacionista*.

A series of factors led to the defeat of the PLN at the polls in 1958. The already cited rise in consumer prices and a split in the ranks of the party were undoubtedly the two principal ones. The victor in the 1958 presidential race was Mario Echandi, who led a coalition of Ulate's National Union Party (PUN) and the *calderonista* party. This coalition of the enemies of the 1948 revolution in the election of a decade later is perhaps the clearest evidence of the transition of the PRN away from a concern with the welfare of Costa Rica's working class. Since 1958 the PRN has been even more personalistic-oriented than it was in the 1940–48 period, when it was the official party of the country. The years of the Echandi administration can chiefly be characterized as a period when the PLN program, begun during the Figueres junta of 1948 and 1949 and continued during Don "Pepe's" term as president, was slowed

4 Ibid., pp. 17–18.

down or brought to a stop. Between 1958 and 1962 government intervention in the economy was curbed, and no new programs of economic development were commenced. During this period per capita income in Costa Rica actually decreased. Most notable of Echandi's policies was his resolution to keep Costa Rica out of the newly formed Central American Common Market, undoubtedly a resolution well supported by his oligarchic supporters.

In 1962 the PRN pitted party leader and former president Calderón against losing 1958 PLN presidential candidate Francisco Orlich, a party moderate. Former president Otílio Ulate ran as a candidate of the PUN. Acting in combination the PRN and PUN have been able to oppose effectively the PLN and its organization at the polls. However, running candidates of their own, the *calderonistas* and the *ulatistas* were not able to stand up to Orlich and the reunified PLN. In addition to restoring the PLN programs and returning the government to its prime role as problem solver in the society, the Orlich administration took Costa Rica into the Central American Common Market and established a Central Planning Office.

The 1966 election found the PLN retaining its slim majority in the National Assembly, but losing the presidential office to a candidate of the PUN-PRN coalition. Having learned from the election of 1962 that neither of their organizations could defeat the PLN by running separate tickets, *calderonista* and *ulatista* leaders formed a joint ticket in 1966 which led to the victory of university economics professor José Joaquín Trejos Fernandez.

Trejos's term in office seemed to be characterized by a return to the incrementalist problem-solving styles and the stopgap policies of the Echandi administration. Sales taxes were increased, the currency was unofficially devaluated, and a concerted effort was made to dilute the already weak power of such agencies as the National Office of Planning and the Agrarian Reform Institute.

Five candidates ran for office in the election of 1970. The victor was José "Pepe" Figueres, founder of the PLN and revolutionary hero, who called for new efforts to tackle his country's development problems. Figueres's principal opponent, candidate of the National Unification Party, the *calderonista-ulatista* group, was Mario Echandi, also a former president. One factor which did work against the latter was a minor split in the *anti-liberacionista* group which he headed. Led by 1966–70 second vice-president

Virgilio Calvo, the so-called National Front polled a tiny fraction of the total votes cast. Younger members of the *calderonista* group clustered around Calvo, forming a highly personalistic organization, while their mentors, tired of the strife and having learned from past defeats, remained loyal to Echandi. For the first time, Costa Rica's Christian Democratic party fielded a candidate for the presidency in the person of Jorge Monge, who received even fewer votes than Calvo. Socialist Action, a tiny party which includes many of the old *Vanguardia Popular* membership among its followers, performed in about the same fashion as did the other two minority parties.

SUMMARY

Recent Costa Rican political and economic history has been dominated by an ideology and program promoted by a single political party—the Figueres-founded PLN. Its victory at the polls in 1970 served to confirm this. Recognizing that the government is the most likely problem solver for the economically underdeveloped society as a whole, when in power the PLN has undertaken to resolve some of the difficulties faced by Costa Rica. The PLN has viewed the bureaucracy as the instrumentality of government which is most likely to be capable of tackling development problems and has strengthened it accordingly. Every effort has been made to remove the bureaucracy from the political arena; the effects of this policy are discussed below. At the same time the PLN has shown a remarkable concern for civil liberties and, of course, for all of the trappings of what is termed democratic government. The PLN's policies and programs are examined in this and other chapters below. Most important to note here, however, is that this party is the only organization in Costa Rica with an integrated program of development for the country. As will be seen, for a variety of reasons the Figueres plan and program has often not been implemented; and, when it has, it has not met adequately with many of the problems faced by the Central American republic.

The Formal Institutions

As is the case in other Latin American countries, in the formal and legalistic sense Costa Rican politics resemble those of the United

States. The governmental structures of the Central American nation are in many ways modeled on those of its neighbor in North America. The government is presidential in form; the executive, legislative, and judicial branches are formally separated. As will be discussed below, this separation actually exists in the informal sense as well as in the formal one, an unusual situation in a country of the Latin American area.

THE PRESIDENCY

The president of Costa Rica is elected popularly for a term of four years, and he can occupy this high office only once in his lifetime. A recent constitutional amendment prohibits reelection under any circumstances except for former presidents who served prior to 1966. This is the reason that Figueres and Echandi were permitted to run in the 1970 election. Although there are two vice-presidents, both elected on the same ticket with the president, neither receives any significant responsibilities from his office; and, in the case of the second vice-president, there is no salary attached to the position.

The president is specifically assigned only four functions by the 1949 constitution, a document written at a time when there was great fear of the abuse of executive power in Costa Rica. The four functions are the only ones which he is permitted to perform unilaterally, without the participation of another official such as a cabinet minister or a member of the National Assembly. The president may appoint and remove his ministers, command the national guard (a form of constabulary established after Figueres abolished the military), represent the nation at official ceremonies as its chief of state, and present a state of the union address without the participation in the action of any other official. On the other hand, the president cannot leave the country without the permission of the National Assembly, nor can he exercise the power of the veto without the concurrence of one or more cabinet ministers. There is no item veto. Duties of the president that must be performed jointly with a member or members of the cabinet include the formulation of the national budget, the supervision of the bureaucracy, the appointment of non-civil service public administrators, and the signing of a bill into law.

Besides the limitations on the functions which he may perform, there are other institutional limitations on the power of the Costa

Rican chief executive. The control of the president over the executive branch of the government has been particularly weakened by the National Assembly over the last two decades, which under the leadership of the PLN has created a sizeable group of so-called semiautonomous institutions. In the year 1967, for example, this particular type of institution accounted for 50 percent of the expenditures of the government. These semiautonomous institutions are quite independent of executive controls. Their policies are formed and acted upon by individual boards of directors rather than by the chief executive. Financially most of these institutions are independent as they either have sources of income independent of the chief executive's controls, or, in a few cases, are guaranteed a certain percentage of the national budget. Practically all of the organizations of the public administration charged with bringing change to Costa Rica are independent of each other and of the chief executive.

The president of Costa Rica enjoys no widespread decree authority as do some other Latin American chief executives. This and the above outlined very real limits on the presidency have had profound effects on the political decision-making process as will be seen below.

THE LEGISLATURE

The Costa Rican legislature, known as the National Assembly, is unicameral and in the 1970–74 term was composed of fifty-seven members. The legislators, or deputies, are elected through a system of proportional representation for terms of four years, and they cannot be reelected unless at least one term intervenes after they have served. The National Assembly possesses considerable power when compared to other Latin American legislatures; party discipline is strictly enforced, and issues are sharply debated.

Legislation may be initiated by any member of the legislature or by a cabinet minister representing the president of the republic. Bills are studied by one or possibly two of the five principal standing committees for approximately one week and are then reported back. They then must be debated on three separate days by the full National Assembly, and are passed by a simple majority of those present at the end of the debate. A quorum in Costa Rica's legislature is constituted by two-thirds of the deputies or their elected substitutes. As in many Latin American nations each legislator is elected along with a substitute, and in the days that the former cannot be present, the latter assumes his seat. Thus the empty chambers so characteristic of the United States legislature are avoided in Costa Rica.

There are actually seven standing committees in the National Assembly; however, the Bill Editing Committee and the Legislative Library Committee are of very little importance. The Committees for Judicial Affairs, Social Affairs, Economic Affairs, Budget Affairs, and for Government and Administration are the important of the seven. These are made up of eleven or twelve members who serve on the Committee for one year only. Most of the deputies can look forward to serving on at least four different committees during their terms. Occasionally a deputy will be assigned by the Speaker of the Assembly to remain one extra year on a particular committee, but this is not the norm. There is no specialization or expertise among the deputies as a result of this rotation of assignment process, and there are concomitant limitations on the quality of the work which the legislators produce. The committees have no permanent staff of experts which might help to fill the gaps created by the lack of expertise among the deputies. In some cases experts are available in Costa Rica and are called to testify before one committee or another; but it is a hit-or-miss type of operation when the deputies, limited to one week for their investigations, begin to search for data and information. Most of the deputies do not understand the importance of committee work as far as the goals of the National Assembly are concerned; and, instead of working toward these goals, they use their committee appointments as a method of making contacts in the various interest areas. These contacts are then put to good use when the deputies are out of office.

Significantly, the Costa Rican Bureau of the Budget falls directly under the supervision of the National Assembly and is entirely independent of the president. This was considered by the authors of the 1949 Constitution to be the most effective way of assuring that the office of the chief executive would remain weak. The power of the purse strings was assigned to the legislature. There have been many problems inherent in this arrangement, particularly since fifty-seven persons are assigned to supervise the Bureau of the Budget. The Committee for Budgetary Affairs, with its rotating membership, is not in a very good position to supervise this bureau either. With no budgetary experts at their call, this Committee's membership each year has hardly been in a position to prepare a government budget. In recent years the practice has been for the president to prepare it, while the Assembly spends months primarily debating it before approving it and assigning to the Bureau of the Budget the responsibility for administering it.

Still another legislative responsibility, a practice unusual for many nations, is the appointment of Costa Rican Supreme Court justices. The National Assembly can also create courts, temporarily cancel civil liberties, and engage in a series of related activities.

Legislators play a major role in the amendment of the Costa Rican constitution. A minimum of ten deputies must sign a proposed amendment, regardless of its actual initiator, and submit it to the Assembly. The amendment must be debated during two separate annual sessions. After debate during the first year it is voted upon; in order for it to pass, two-thirds of the total membership of the legislature must approve it. The amendment is then forwarded to the president, who considers it, returning it to the National Assembly with his comments the following year. The legislators can choose to ignore the comments made by the president. Once again the amendment is voted upon, and if it receives a two-thirds majority vote, it becomes a part of the Constitution. Under no circumstances can a president veto an amendment or any portion of it.

Despite its apparent powers the National Assembly is as limited as is the president in its ability to carry out its functions. The fact that the deputies cannot seek reelection until a four-year term intervenes tends to limit the continuity of the body and discourages specialization in particular policy-making areas. The committee system, with its revolving membership, assures that most issues will be acted upon in a piecemeal fashion and on the basis of limited information. Proportional representation, which will be examined in more detail in the next chapter, has meant that it is difficult for any one party to win a majority of the legislative seats. In the last three National Assembly terms, the majority party, the PLN, has maintained its place by a single vote. Despite the strong party discipline that is characteristic of the National Assembly, this is a thin edge indeed.

THE JUDICIARY

The judicial branch of the Costa Rican government is less central to decision making than are the other two formal national government branches. This does not mean, however, that the judiciary is any less independent than are the other two. The seventeen justices of the Supreme Court are appointed by the National Assembly for terms of eight years. The terms are staggered, and few are appointed during any one election year. The Court can rule on the constitutionality of executive and legislative actions, including laws passed and presidential vetoes.

The Supreme Court is the only court to which a Costa Rican citizen can appeal for the right of *habeas corpus* and for the broader writ of *amparo*. The distinction between the two writs is that in the former the citizen, after having been placed under arrest, appeals to the Supreme Court to set him free, while in the latter the citizen, not under detention, appeals for the restoration of any civil liberty, such as freedom of speech, of which he feels that he has been deprived.

LOCAL GOVERNMENT

The seven provinces of Costa Rica are simply administrative subdivisions of the central government. The provinces are divided into cantons which do display some degree of semiautonomy from the government in San José. Each canton popularly elects a council which meets on a regular basis to consider such things as the maintenance of roads and certain other minor problems. The head of the council is not elected, however, but instead is appointed by the president. In the case of a tie in a council vote the president's appointee casts the deciding vote. In practice a great deal of the agenda is prepared by the council head.

THE BUREAUCRACY

As has been noted, the public administration of Costa Rica has expanded rapidly in the last two decades, a growth rate unmatched even by the country's spectacularly mushrooming population. The growth of the bureaucracy has been neither controlled nor planned; organizations vary widely even in the regular nonautonomous agencies. There is no career ladder and a considerable overlapping of functions occurs between the various agencies; empire building is a common trait of top administrators. The result of this uncoordinated growth has been a stopgap and piecemeal policy-making process and indirectly a slow evolution toward greater autonomy in all branches of government. Since this growth has been occurring hand-in-hand with a greater emphasis on government as a problem solver for the entire society, a considerable amount of dissatisfaction could be expected both within and without the bureaucracy. On the part of the bureaucrats themselves, this does not appear to be the case. From one study it would appear that the relative youthfulness of the administrators has worked against a great deal of cynicism and dissatisfaction arising within the bureaucracy to date.[5]

Contributing to the inflexibility of Costa Rica's relatively new bureaucracy are a series of other factors. One of these, the lack of power on the part of the chief executive, has already been discussed. Another factor is constituted by the civil service system adopted by the government in the mid-1950s as a result of prestige class pressures and the encouragement of several international agencies. By conventional standards this system is the most advanced in the Central American area. Approximately 95 percent of Costa Ricans working in the executive branch of government are covered by civil service. The small percentage who are not are either the tiny group of top officials appointed by the president or a larger group of blue-collar workers who also are employed on the basis of a spoils system. Many of the semiautonomous institutions are beginning to provide at least some semblance of job security to their employees.

Although from the viewpoint of the white-collar prestige class of Costa Rica the introduction of civil service is an agreeable situation, it places severe checks on the bureaucracy. Civil service insures that if a bureaucrat's position is found to be superfluous because of new needs or goals, he cannot be removed. The system limits an already weak chief executive by restricting his appointment and removal powers to the one or two topmost officials in each government organization and a sizeable group of working class individuals at the bottom of each hierarchy. The large group of policy imple-

[5] Charles F. Denton, "The Politics of Development in Costa Rica," (Ph.D. diss., The University of Texas at Austin, January, 1969).

menters from the prestige class are independent of the president. In general the civil service system has not insured a more efficient public administration, but instead has helped to maintain the bureaucratic status quo. Civil service has reinforced the lack of coordination and the overlapping of functions which is characteristic of the Costa Rican public administration and has assured that there will be some excess of employees working for the government.

Of course the conceptualization of an excess of employees is wholly arbitrary, based on efficiency input-output criteria. If the bureaucracy is regarded as a tension management device for the social system rather than as a problem solver, then the large number of government employees with job security may be desirable.

One of the most significant characteristics of the Costa Rican bureaucracy is its tendency to disintegrate into semiautonomy; witness the large number of semiautonomous institutions already in existence there. These institutions have had profound effects on administrative practice on the one hand and the entire political process on the other. Costa Rica has taken to the use of semiautonomous institutions in its public administration with a greater alacrity than probably any Latin American nation. These agencies, which with a few exceptions have grown up since the *liberacionista* revolution of 1948, appear to be a direct result of the ideological commitment of the PLN leadership to democratic ideas and procedures, such as checks and balances. An example of the ideology has been presented at the beginning of the chapter, and this concern with civil liberties has permeated the entire governmental structure. So great is the fear of strong government, or of any governmental agency gaining strength in relation to others, that every effort has been made to balance them off; for example, it is difficult to determine whether the chief executive or the legislature has more decision-making strength in Costa Rica. The semiautonomous institutions are simply one more symptom of this *liberacionista* and prestige-class concern with checking and balancing their government.

Since the ratification of the constitution of 1949, written after the *liberacionista* revolution, the Costa Rican government has been charged with the responsibility of establishing "semiautonomous" agencies of the bureaucracy to assume specific developmental or technical tasks assigned to them by the National Assembly. The semiautonomous agencies were ordered to direct the economy and society of Costa Rica in such a fashion as to bring change in a "nonpolitical" manner. The result of this emphasis on autonomy in the change-oriented institutions of the bureaucracy has actually been a clouding of the policy-making process rather than the removal of development efforts from the political arena.

Most of the boards of directors of the semiautonomous institutions are appointed in off-election years for periods ranging from four to six years. The policies of the institutions are formed and decided by the boards of directors rather than by a particular political organization. In some cases the boards of directors name the prospective managers of their institutions, who are then confirmed by the president. The legislature, including its standing committee on government and administration, has nothing to say about the nomination or confirmation of appointments in the semiautonomous agencies. The president appoints members of the boards of directors over a staggered period without consultation with the legislative assembly. However, the directors cannot be removed by the president once he has appointed them.

In financial matters most of the semiautonomous institutions are independent, as either they have sources of income independent of the chief executive or the National Assembly's Bureau of the Budget or, in a few cases, are guaranteed a certain percentage of the annual budget by law or by constitutional provision. The University of Costa Rica, one example of a semiautonomous institution, is guaranteed 5 percent of the budget by law. The Agrarian Reform Institute sells bananas on the international market and rents or leases portions of the country's seashores and national parks for its revenues. The banks lend money, the electrical institute sells energy, and the Pacific Railway sells space; each uses its revenues to continue its own program independently.

With the rapid growth of the semiautonomous institutions, which spend an average 50 percent of all government expenditures annually, a difficult situation has developed. Virtually all of the public administrative organizations responsible for bringing change to the Central American nation are independent of each other and of the chief executive. There is little or no budgetary control. Since these institutions represent the main problem-solving apparatus of Costa Rica, it is safe to assert that national problems are being tackled in what is at best a piecemeal fashion.

Another difficulty facing Costa Rica's public administration is a general lack of economic resources. Since taxation efforts have never been able to provide sufficient operating funds, there is a perpetual shortage of revenues in the case of those agencies with no independent sources of income. This has led the nonautonomous agencies to find new ways to raise money, whether it be the selling of stamps, legal paper, or charging fees for particular services rendered. As the nonautonomous agencies develop new sources of income, they begin to achieve more independence from the chief executive and the National Assembly. It is interesting to note that despite the perpetual economic shortage in the bureaucracy the civil service system includes a pension plan which provides excellent benefits both to public servants and their dependents. Seventeen different programs of retirement are offered to Costa Rica's public administrators, all of them elaborate and expensive. For a government which is always in the throes of one economic crisis or another, these expensive payments can lead only to less solvency and the need to borrow more from abroad.

SUMMARY

Costa Rica displays an elaborate set of checked-and-balanced governmental institutions, particularly considering the size, social structure, and economic resources of the country. The question can be preliminarily asked as to what effects a governmental system such as the one in Costa Rica can have on what is essentially an agrarian society and which is characterized by a highly non-participant and nonequalitarian social system. There is a school of thought which proposes that the establishment of "democratic" government similar to the one in the United States is a surefire method for bringing change to any of the Latin American countries. Briefly it should be stated here that the overall picture of Costa Rica's government is one of immobilism. Each of the branches of government is quite capable of checking the others if they attempt to innovate or to change very much in their environment. In a negative sense the formal government structures, including the bureaucracy, are quite powerful. Clearly the system is designed, consciously or unconsciously, to preserve things the way they are. A governmental system such as this one in a country with limited resources is clearly not advantageous to change.

However, prior to reaching conclusions of this sort about the Costa Rican system, it is necessary to view other political institutions and the processes which interact within and without them. The concluding section of this chapter examines some of the non-governmental political institutions of the country with emphasis on how they relate to the preceding analysis.

Other Political Institutions

In most Latin American countries the most important political institution is actually one portion of the bureaucracy: the military, which controls the use of violence, has assumed a preeminent position in this Hemisphere. This is not the case in Costa Rica. As noted above, "Pepe" Figueres took an unusual step in abolishing the military of his country after the revolution of 1948. The military organization had abused its power prior to that date partly, it must be admitted, at the prompting of the *calderonistas*; this had given rise to a general revulsion toward authority, particularly uniformed authority. The white-collar prestige class groups, who had their shops and enterprises sacked by the army during the lockout of 1947, were able to gain sufficient influence so as to permit them to bring about the virtual elimination of the military.

The reaction against the military has been so strong that even in the 1960s, when because of a rising crime rate there has been a demand for more protection for private citizens, this type of demand is directed away from the political system. The inexpert national guard or constabulary, which experiences a major shift in its manpower after each election, has served to reinforce the general impression that the government should not be more than minimally involved in the prevention of crime. The changeover in personnel at each election is so great that it is estimated that within six months after a new president assumes offices, 90 percent of the men from the previous guard have been removed and replaced by political appointees. Since the abolition of the army in 1948, the presidency has changed hands every four years with a similar complete change in civil guard manpower. As can be gathered from this data, the constabulary, which in 1965 received less than 4 percent of total government expenditures in that year, is a major source of presidential spoils and has been used by each party to reward its faithful.

The men who survive a change in regime in the military are not the officer corps but are usually a motley personnel. No seniority is built up over four years. Those who do survive may make tremendous jumps or drops in rank with the arrival in office of a new president. It is not unusual to find a man who has been promoted from the rank of private to lieutenant or captain, for example. The effects of this situation on morale, on efficiency, and on organizational strength are not difficult to fathom. Costa Rica makes no pretense that the National Guard can defend the country in case of an attack from abroad; the country has formally passed the defense responsibilities over to the Organization of American States. Crime is a mounting problem. But the limits on the Guard's capability for engaging in political intervention are as important. As long as the Guard remains a major source of presidential spoils, the chance that it will carry out some form of formal or informal coup d'etat appears to be very remote.

Another institution of considerable importance in many Latin American countries is the Roman Catholic Church. The Church is involved in all aspects of national life—sociocultural, economic, and political. As mentioned previously, secularization is only minimally advanced in Costa Rica. Although church attendance is usually reserved for women and children, the influence of the organization is much more far-reaching, particularly as far as rules made by political decision makers pertaining to marriage and the family are concerned. The Church does not normally participate as an innovator of rules, but it can become actively involved in defending existing ones. For example, divorce laws are strict, and the knowledge that there would be strong opposition by the Church to any proposed change making them more lenient has been sufficient to block any such proposals.

Evidence of the Church's involvement in all aspects of the national life is abundant. Religious instruction is obligatory for all children in the state-operated public school system. Non-Roman Catholics can be excused from these periods, but the peer group sanctions imposed on these students makes it difficult for them to leave the classroom when a member of the clergy arrives. No public road or building is ever inaugurated without the participation of a member of the clergy. If the item to be dedicated is sufficiently important, water from the Jordan River in the Middle East is used to dedicate the project. The Church has operated labor unions; and one priest, Padre Benjamín Núñez, served as a director of the *Institute Nacional de Vivienda y Urbanismo* (INVU), the national housing institute, from 1966 to 1970. Franking privileges and actual subsidy payments to the Church, as exist in certain of the Latin American nations, have been eliminated in Costa Rica.

The political parties of Costa Rica are treated in the following chapter. As can be inferred from the historical sketch above, the parties range from the personalistic to the program-oriented.

INTEREST GROUPS

One of the most prominent and certainly the most influential interest group in Costa Rica is the *Asociación Nacional de Fomento Económico* (ANFE). With a relatively small membership—only about three hundred persons belonged to the organization in 1968—its size is no indication of its political influence. Members include business and industrial leaders, politicians, bureaucrats, educators, and even a cabinet member in the 1966–70 Trejos administration. Ideologically, ANFE's position is close to the theories of the nineteenth-century Manchesterian laissez–faire economic liberals, a stance almost the opposite of the ones held by "Pepe" Figueres and his *liberacionistas*. There are very few of the latter amongst the membership of the ANFE.

ANFE consistently maintains what, for lack of a better term, can be called a far-right position on economic and political issues and vociferously publicizes its views in the press and at regular meetings. Costa Rica's leading newspaper, *La Nación*, carries a column in each issue written by one or another official of the organization. It also sponsors regular meetings for university students and others to put across its viewpoints. With an annual operating budget of thirty thousands dollars, a permanent staff of three, and a large headquarters including a well-stocked library, ANFE is undoubtedly one of Costa Rica's most active and well-known interest groups.

ANFE, which is certainly better organized and equipped than either the *calderonista* or *ulatista* parties, publicly rejects any efforts by the government to solve the country's socioeconomic problems. At the same time its businessmen and industrialist members are reasonably certain that the government is not likely to eliminate the high tariff wall erected to protect them or to withdraw other special incentives now proffered to them. There is still another reason for ANFE's laissez–faire stance. Leaders of the organization believe that if it vociferously promotes a very far right position on all issues, individuals who only partially oppose government problem-solving efforts and the PLN program will appear moderate in the eyes of many.

The ANFE organization has loaned its talents and publicity outlets to the *calderonista-ulatista* coalition during recent election campaigns but has specifically avoided presenting candidates for office or becoming labeled as a political party. Whether ANFE leader Trino Araya Borge, who once trucked ammunition to the *liberacionista* forces during the 1948 revolution, will decide to run for office—using his organization as a stepping-stone—is difficult to determine.

A rather bizarre Costa Rican interest group is the *Movimiento Costa Rica Libre* (MCRL). This group announces to all concerned that its sole purpose for existing is to combat communism in Costa Rica. With a membership of approximately a thousand, this group specializes in training youth in the arts of antiguerrilla warfare. The MCRL has cached weapons in the countryside and supposedly boasts a membership capable of using them. It frequently publishes anticommunist advertisements in the press and sponsors regular meetings, some public and others of a more clandestine nature. No active politicians currently belong to this group, and the MCRL, like ANFE, restricts itself to endorsing certain candidates during election campaigns. The basic purpose of the group—as stated regularly in the newspapers of San José—is to meet the communists on any ground they care to fight upon. As will be discussed, the communist movement in Costa Rica is miniscule in activity, program, and membership; the MCRL, however, in a classic witch-hunting fashion, believes that many in the PLN and the government, as well as all the *calderonistas*, are communists.

MCRL leader, Guillermo Castro Echeverría, who holds a Bronze Star for valor won while fighting with the United States Army during World War II, heads the private army maintained by his organization and is its political boss as well. This private army is one of two which operate in Costa Rica; the other belongs to politician Frank Marshall Jiménez and will be discussed in the succeeding chapter. Castro has held several offices in the government, but whether he aspires to a political position won through the efforts of his organization is difficult to determine.

All teachers and professors in the Costa Rican public school system, which includes the university, are members of the National Association of Educators (ANDE). In 1963 membership numbered some thirteen thousand persons, and it would seem probable that increases have occurred since then. Upon assuming a teaching post in the public school system, a teacher automatically becomes a member of ANDE; membership dues are deducted from a teacher's paychecks. Costa Rica has been proud of the fact that since 1948 it has numbered more teachers than soldiers in its population. Regular income, coupled with the prestige allocated to educators and the fact that many teaching professionals use their jobs as springboards into politics or the public administration, has assured the ANDE a powerful political voice. The organization has managed to drive teacher salary scales upward, if not to a comfortable level, at least sufficiently to match rises in living costs. Since most teachers, like other professionals of the prestige class, hold down other jobs in addition to their teaching, most of the educators are capable of maintaining a living standard equitable with their social status. Interestingly, ANDE, an upper social sector, white-collar organization, is the only effective union in Costa Rica—although it would definitely reject the nomenclature—for it also lobbies for improved schools and textbooks. Incoming chief executives have learned the necessity of consulting with ANDE prior to appointing a Minister of Education.

Costa Rican students have not been as politically influential as have their mentors, nor does their participation and interest compare to their counterparts in the United States and other Latin American countries. Students at the university usually belong either to the *Federación de Estudiantes Costarricenses* (FECR) or to the youth wing of the PLN. Some inroads have been made on the campus by the Christian Democratic political organization. The students have become involved in political disputes on rare occasions, but usually only when the issue actually concerns them, as in 1967 when the National Assembly determined to reduce the percentage of the national budget which the university automatically receives each year. When a strike was declared by the students and marches held, the legislators backed down under the pressure.

And, as in other Latin American countries, a bus-fare increase usually sparks student demonstrations; unlike their affluent counterparts in the United States, most Costa Rican university students do not travel to classes by automobile.

Perhaps the principal reason that students in Costa Rica are not involved more actively in the politics of their country as a group is their relatively advanced age at the time they attend. Most have waited several years after graduation from high school to gain admission to the university; the average entering freshman is twenty-two years of age. Working part time, attending class part time means that a thirty-year-old graduate is not at all unusual. By the time they attend the university in Costa Rica, students have already become committed to the socioeconomic system by their jobs and families. If they participate in politics, it is as representatives of some other group that they do so.

The National Association of Public Servants (ANEP) lists only some 5 percent of all government employees, mostly at the blue-collar level, on its membership lists. Since most bureaucrats belong to the civil service system, the growth of ANEP has been stunted. Periodic wage increases, the reduction of work hours, job security, and the payment of the *aguinaldo*, or a thirteenth month of salary at Christmas, are guaranteed to all but the politically appointed blue-collar workers of the Costa Rican public administration. Also working against the ANEP are its shifting membership and the fact that decision makers know that it speaks for very few of the bureaucrats. ANEP does operate a credit union which is available to members and nonmembers; its income from this operation has enabled it to continue to operate.

Costa Rican labor unions have always been political by nature. *Vanguardia Popular*, the powerful communist-dominated organization of the 1940s, participated actively in politics until proscribed in 1951. It has now more or less disappeared, since it no longer is capable of providing benefits to labor. The only other labor union organization with any strength, Padre Benjamín Núnez's *Rerum Novarum* Union, was founded as a Christian answer to the communist-dominated *Vanguardia Popular*. *Rerum Novarum* disappeared shortly after the demise of its competitor. Núnez supposedly merged his organization with the prestige class-oriented PLN party, but the alliance clearly worked to the advantage of upper-sector interests both within and without the party. When the PLN is in control of the executive branch of the government, it raises the minimum wage every two years, but the wage does not seem to be enforced anywhere in the country. Inspectors are few and jobs are scarce, so the less-than-scrupulous employer does not need to feel bound by the minimum wage legislation. After *Rerum Novarum* was merged with the PLN in 1953, there remained no major independent union in Costa Rica. By 1968, in the entire republic only one collective bargaining contract remained in force; this was an agreement between banana workers and their United Fruit Company employers. The PLN used the strength of labor to propel itself into the political arena, but has since neglected it. Little wonder then that the laboring class of the cities has supported *calderonista-ulatista* candidates in some recent elections.

A number of smaller upper-sector groups—organizations which present one particular type of demand or support to political decision makers—are worthy of consideration in this context. The Chamber of Coffee Growers, potentially a powerful group because of the important role this crop plays in the export market, is limited in its political influence because of wide disagreements on policy among its membership. In addition to this, there are so many coffee growers in Costa Rica, each desirous of selling his crop in the United States-allocated quota, that these farmers tend to undercut each other politically in order to reach the rich American market. One of the goals of the Chamber of Coffee Growers is to convince the United States to pay more per pound for Costa Rican coffee. If every American would be willing to pay just one cent more per cup of coffee, so the Chamber logic runs, Costa Rica could be transformed economically in just a few years. The Chamber has been no more successful in dealing with United States decision makers than it has with their Costa Rican counterparts.

The Dairy Farmers' Association and the Chamber of Commerce are two organizations quite similar to the Chamber of Coffee Growers, although the influence of the latter has been eclipsed by the ANFE. In fact, it would appear that most of the members of all three groups funnel their political demands either through ANFE or through one or another political party.

In an interesting way the United States Agency for International Development (AID) can be termed a Costa Rican political interest group. In return for its capital, badly needed by the government to balance its budget, AID demands that certain rules and regulations be adopted by the Costa Ricans. AID lobbies both directly and indirectly for its programs through the press and by talking to political decision makers. For example, in the late 1960s representatives of the AID were pressing publicly and privately for more effective taxation processes and for a career military service. The former demand is being met gradually, while it seems highly unlikely that Costa Rican decision makers will accede to the latter, given the nature of public opinion against men in uniform.

INTERNATIONAL INTERESTS

Although not specifically interest groups, two other organizations have had considerable influence on the political process in Costa Rica. One is the United Nations-established Central American School of Public Administration (ESAPAC), while the other is the Inter-American School of Political Education. The former has had significant influence over the formation of the bureaucracy in Costa Rica, while the latter has contributed to the formation of the PLN ideology and program.

The Inter-American School of Political Education was founded in the 1950s by the so-called League of Social Democratic Parties of Latin America. This League, which is actually a very loosely tied group, includes the PLN, APRA of Peru, Acción Democrática of Venezuela, the Movimiento Nacional Revolucionario of Bolivia, and the Febrerista Party of Paraguay among others. It is interesting to note that for several years primary support came from the United States Central Intelligence Agency, which between 1961 and 1964, for example, funneled $258,000 into the school.[6] The Inter-American School of Political Education, located twenty miles outside of San José, has now been converted into an Institute of Cooperative Education. But until 1968 the school had contributed to the indoctrination of several hundred Latin American youth leaders including members of the PLN. Significantly, other members of this League of Social Democratic Parties have felt the Costa Rican organization to be the least ideologically oriented of their number and point to the PLN's domestic program as ample evidence of this allegation. The fact that Costa Rica provided a tiny contingent of

[6] Dan Kurzman, "Labor Group Got $1 Million From CIA," *Washington Post*, February 21, 1967, p. 1. According to Kurzman the funds were funneled through the J. M. Kaplan Fund of New York and Norman Thomas' Institute for International Labor Research.

troops to the interventionist force during the 1965 Dominican crisis while PLN President Francisco Orlich was in office has not helped the case of the Costa Rican organization in the eyes of its peers. This league did influence the formation of PLN ideology through the years and did contribute to the education of various *liberacionista* leaders.

The United Nation's ESAPAC has played a major role in the establishment of regional organizations working toward the integration of the Central American isthmus. It has been a prime mover in the establishment of civil service in Costa Rica, an institution which is not wholly beneficial to the development of the country. The director of the ESAPAC is an active supporter of the PLN, has served in various government positions when that party has been in control of the executive office, and has lectured at the Inter-American School of Political Education. He has had, as a result, a direct influence on administrative practice in Costa Rica. The director has advocated central planning and was able, along with other United Nations experts, to convince President Francisco Orlich of the PLN to establish a National Office of Planning. The director has long advocated efficiency in administration; and, largely as a result of his efforts, the central department of the Planning Office is called the Department of Administrative Efficiency. As has already been discussed, there are some inherent contradictions in advocating both a civil service system and efficiency in the bureaucracy of a country such as Costa Rica.

Summary

For a country as small as Costa Rica to have as elaborate a set of political institutions, both formal and informal, is highly unusual, particularly considering its limited resources. Maurice Duverger has stated that in practice it is impossible to apply a pluralist system where the greater part of the population is hungry and generally lacking in educational facilities.[7] According to the French political scientist, democratic processes only prolong the existence of gross inequalities and economic and social underdevel-

[7] Maurice Duverger, *The Idea of Politics* (Indianapolis: Bobbs-Merrill, 1964), p. 101.

opment by camouflaging them. In effect he is arguing that the introduction of political institutions similar to those of the United States and Western Europe will not lead to change in the economically underdeveloped societies.

The population of Costa Rica is only relatively hungry, but with a per capita income of four hundred dollars it is not affluent by any means. And Duverger's second criterion would certainly apply to Costa Rica: as has been noted, although everyone does receive a modicum of education, enough to make them functionally literate, the great majority of them never progress beyond the fourth grade. The final chapter of the volume examines the problem presented by Duverger by attempting to determine what sort of political process emerges when a pluralistic set of political institutions are applied to the economically underdeveloped and nonequalitarian society which is Costa Rica. The final chapter also assesses whether these institutions and the processes which have grown up around them tend to perpetuate the socioeconomic status quo or whether they are bringing change to Costa Rican society, as the creator of much of the political apparatus—the PLN—claims they are. Before examining this problem, however, it is necessary to assess the Costa Rican party system in some detail, as well as its relationship to the electoral system and voting behavior. This analysis is contained in the succeeding chapter.

4

The Political Party System and Voting Behavior

The analysis of each of the Costa Rican political parties below is designed to shed some light on their potential for bringing change to the systems in which they operate. Although it would appear that emphasis has been placed on the PLN, the fact that it is the only political party with a permanent organization makes it mandatory to devote more space to the consideration of it. The second part of this chapter contains an analysis of the Costa Rican electoral system with particular emphasis on the effect that it has had on party formation. And, finally, voting behavior is considered. Since voting is probably the only participation in decision making enjoyed by the majority of the population, it is of importance.

As will be intimated throughout this chapter, it is the socio-economic and ideological environment of the Costa Rican party system that has had primary influence on its formation, rather than technical factors such as the nature of the Supreme Tribunal of Elections (TSE) or the use of proportional representation in voting. The party system has evolved because of the need to meet certain demands, to control others, and to give as many persons of the prestige class participation in decision making about the scarce resources of their country as possible. One group found it necessary to strike up an alliance with certain working-class groups temporarily, but this did not imply that the nonstatus side of the alliance obtained access to participation. In fact, in the final analysis it meant less participation for the working class when certain elements of labor merged with the PLN.

THE NATIONAL LIBERATION PARTY

The National Liberation Party (PLN) is often labeled by analysts of the Latin American areas as a strongly ideological organization.[1] There is no doubt that the PLN does espouse an ideology which is vaguely referred to as "social democracy" and which has permitted it to be a member of the League of Social Democratic Parties of Latin America. In fact, this ideology is one of the factors which in the past has distinguished the PLN from other Costa Rican political parties. But this ideology has been somewhat diluted during the PLN quests for electoral office, and the party has been marked by a strong vein of personalism surrounding the person of José "Pepe" Figueres, victor in the 1970 election, diminutive hero of the revolution, noted international writer and lecturer, and past president of his country. There have been times when ideology or program have been placed in a position of greater importance than certain personalities and gaining office—witness the party's defeat in the election of 1966—but gradually this situation has changed. Unlike other Latin American Social Democratic Organizations which have remained perpetually out of office, like APRA of Peru and Paraguay's Febrerista Party, the PLN is characterized by a strong degree of pragmatism which makes gaining office of extreme importance. And, like so many of the other social democratic parties, the PLN is still dominated by a single individual: the fact that "Pepe" ran for the presidency in the 1970 election demonstrates his continuing importance in the political mainstream of the *liberacionista* organization.

Background. In April, 1940, a group of students and professors at the newly founded University of Costa Rica established what became known as the "Center of National Studies." Among the founders of this "Center" were many of the men who later formed part of the PLN leadership. The group met on a regular basis to discuss politics and the development needs of their country—the depression was still in full swing in Costa Rica. The group published several tracts; and, as certain members became dissatisfied with the *calderonista* government, they began to engage in sporadic

[1] See, for example, Charles W. Anderson, "Politics and Development Policy in Central America," *Midwest Journal of Political Science* 5, No. 4 (November, 1961), 332–50.

sabotage. The members of the Center were revolutionary minded and ideological in their orientation.

In 1945 during the government of Teodoro Picado, the Center of National Studies merged with a political splinter group known as "Acción Democrática," which included "Pepe" Figueres and 1962–66 President Francisco Orlich in its membership. The two groups formed the *Partido Social Demócrata*, which stepped up its attack on the *calderonistas*. This organization played a leading role in organizing and encouraging the general strike which created such a crisis in 1947.

In 1948 the *Partido Social Demócrata* backed Otílio Ulate in his presidential race against Dr. Rafael Calderón Guardia. The events of this year, the revolution led by Figueres, and his subsequent victory have been recounted in the previous chapter. The Figueres-organized National Liberation Movement, which included the *Partido Social Demócrata* and the *ulatistas*, broke up soon after victory over the *calderonistas*. The *ulatistas*, which were largely a group of the old-line oligarchy, became disenchanted with the call for social revolution and for government intervention in the economy advocated by Figueres and his followers. The National Liberation Movement, the *Partido Social Demócrata*, and several other groups were formally merged in 1951 into the *Partido Liberación Nacional* (PLN), the present name of the party.

Ideology. On October 12, 1951, the various groups which had led the revolution against Calderón and his followers, founded the PLN.[2] In the *Carta Fundamental*, which was produced at that time, a great deal of what has become party doctrine was developed, consolidated, and printed. Of primary importance to the writers of this document was the acknowledgment of the state as the institution charged with promoting the general welfare of the society as a whole.[3] This concept provided the ideological framework within which the PLN began actively to expand the government's scope of activities and to found the numerous semiautonomous institutions responsible for bringing change to Costa Rica.

In the *Carta Fundamental*, party ideologues defined what they meant by the general welfare. According to the document, the gen-

[2] Daniel Oduber, *Una campaña* (San José: Editorial Eloy Morua Carrillo, 1967).

[3] Partido Liberación Nacional, *Carta Fundamental*, 5–10.

eral welfare means that each individual has the right to the highest possible standard of living, but the state must not violate human dignity in attempting to achieve this economic growth. The quotation from onetime party general secretary Luis Alberto Monge at the beginning of chapter 3 is only one manifestation of this ideology. PLN party ideologues did not and do not foresee the potential dichotomy between socioeconomic growth on the one hand and the protection of civil liberties on the other, as outlined by Duverger and cited above.[4] As a partial result of their oversight, the Costa Rican government, which appears to be one of the most interventionist in Latin America, is actually having only minor effects on its social and economic environments.

Party ideologues regard, as outlined in the *Carta Fundamental*, democracy as the most likely manner for achieving the general welfare. The elaborately checked-and-balanced government and set of political institutions which has grown up in their country and labeled as institutionalized social democracy is considered by them as being a principal catalyst for change. Still another tenet of the PLN ideology is that full employment and high productivity must be societal goals. Under this principle if consistently high levels of production are achieved, then everyone in the country will be employed to keep production moving. However, the balance between the two goals is particularly difficult to maintain in a society such as Costa Rica, which has scarce resources. For the tendency will be to provide all with jobs even if they are not needed in the scheme of things. In the Costa Rican bureaucracy the conflict over the goal of high employment and productivity has been particularly noticeable, as discussed in the previous chapter. Work is considered to be a social function; and it is an inherent right, rather than a privilege, for a man to have a job under PLN ideology. The state has the responsibility to maintain the dignity of work and to insure that everyone has a job. Since the prestige class is the one most capable of placing pressure on decision makers and since the government is most capable of providing jobs in its own agencies, the bureaucracy has grown rapidly since the PLN formulated this ideology. As already discussed, this employment-providing function has interfered with the ability of the bureaucracy to cope with Costa Rica's developmental needs.

[4] Duverger, *The Idea of Politics*, p. 101.

One analyst has described the PLN as altruistic in its philosophy, Keynsian in its economic theory, and liberal democratic in its politics.[5] With its limited resources and numerous economic and social problems, there is some doubt as to whether a liberal democratic political philosophy and Keynsian economic theory is suitable for Costa Rica. Both are mild and incrementalist in their approach, while the country's population is growing in what can almost be termed a wild fashion, with no corresponding growth in the availability of economic resources.

The Organization. The National Liberation Party is the only major Costa Rican political party with a permanent organizational structure which extends from the national to the local levels of the country. Each regional division of the country has a PLN committee to boast of. The Figueres organization is also the only major party which provides for and permits individual memberships. Membership in the PLN is divided into three categories. Lowest on the organization's hierarchy are those members who retain what is known as affiliate status. The affiliates are persons who register in writing as supporters of the party and who participate in collective functions such as the local assemblies. The affiliate can, but is not obligated to, contribute financially to the party. Ranking above the affiliates in membership status are the party militants; in addition to participating in the same functions as do the affiliates and registering in writing, the militants must formally and publicly accept the PLN ideology and are assessed regular contributions according to their ability to pay. The highest category of membership is that of leader, a militant member who is elected to one party office or another. Although any militant is qualified to be a leader, the additional status is often made on ascriptive and personalistic bases such as their particular relationship to members of the executive committee. When the party is in power, militants and leaders can usually expect some spoils as a reward for their loyalty and contributions to the party.

The PLN, like all of the established parties in Costa Rica, does not depend on members' dues to cover its operating expenses. The organization receives most of its operating revenues directly from

[5] Donn Scott Smith, "The *Partido Liberación Nacional* of Costa Rica: A Critical Study" (Unpublished manuscript, Woodrow Wilson School of Public and International Affairs, Princeton University, October, 1966).

the government in direct relationship to its performance at the polls. This policy of the Costa Rican government is the result of legislation introduced by the PLN itself in 1949. Any party polling at least 10 percent of the total votes cast in a particular election is entitled to government assistance. The funds are appropriated to each party in proportion to the number of votes which it receives, although subsidies to the PLN and the other political parties cannot exceed the expenses of each organization.

The basic organizational unit of the PLN is the local assembly, made up of affiliates and militants in each canton. The sixty-six local assemblies meet at least once each year and, as elections approach, the gatherings become more frequent. The local assemblies elect ten delegates to the National Party Assembly, which is the supreme body of the PLN. In both the local and the National Assemblies a quorum consists of one-half plus one of the membership.

Each local assembly elects its own executive committee, although candidates for the committee must be militant members of the party. Upon being elected to an executive committee a member immediately achieves leader status in the PLN hierarchy. These local committees meet at least once a month, and their membership serve terms of two years. Members may be removed by a majority of the committee if they miss five consecutive meetings, clearly a liberal attendance policy.

The National Assembly, as shown in Graph 2, is the paramount body of the party. It elects two committees: the Executive Committee, which is formally responsible for the day-to-day operation of the PLN; and a Political Committee, which coordinates campaign activities. In recent years the two committees have usually been characterized by an overlapping membership. Although the National Assembly theoretically reigns supreme in the PLN, it would appear that the Executive Committee is actually the locus of decision making.

The National Assembly does have a variety of duties and these include the approval of a new party program every four years; voting on amendments to the rules and statutes of the party submitted by one or another of the two national committees; selecting the National Party Secretary, who is a paid employee and full-time executive officer of the party; and naming the members of the Na-

Graph 2

PARTIDO LIBERACIÓN NACIONAL

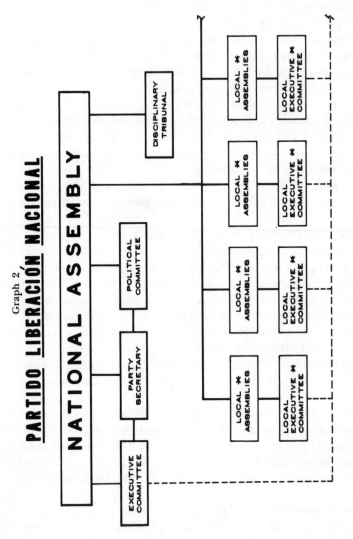

NATIONAL ASSEMBLY

EXECUTIVE COMMITTEE

PARTY SECRETARY

POLITICAL COMMITTEE

DISCIPLINARY TRIBUNAL

LOCAL ASSEMBLIES *

LOCAL EXECUTIVE COMMITTEE *

LOCAL ASSEMBLIES *

LOCAL EXECUTIVE COMMITTEE *

LOCAL ASSEMBLIES *

LOCAL EXECUTIVE COMMITTEE *

LOCAL ASSEMBLIES *

LOCAL EXECUTIVE COMMITTEE *

* THERE IS ONE LOCAL ASSEMBLY AND ONE LOCAL EXECUTIVE COMMITTEE IN EACH OF THE 66 COSTA RICAN CANTONS.

tional Disciplinary Tribunal, who serve for four-year terms. The National Assembly makes binding decisions on all other organs of the party.

Officially it is the Assembly which selects the PLN presidential candidate every four years. Voting for the candidate, by secret ballot, takes place approximately two months before national elections. In order for an aspiring candidate to appear on the primary ballot, he must first attain the status of pre-candidate, a status which is achieved by presenting a petition bearing the signatures of at least two hundred party members to the National Executive Committee. The usual practice has been for the Executive Committee to lend its support to one particular pre-candidate, however, and it is this person who usually achieves victory in the primary balloting. However, in 1958, when a large group of members objected to the choice of the Executive Committee, the PLN split in half during the campaign with the ultimate victory accruing to the ranks of the *anti-liberacionistas*.

The internal working of the PLN, with its numerous opportunities for participation and its well-defined elected hierarchy, appears to be the epitome of equalitarian democracy. However, as suggested above, a great number of decisions are made by the Executive Committee, which may or may not go through the formality of having the party as a whole approve them. Even the agenda for the National Assembly meetings is prepared by the Committee with some participation by key members in the local executive committees. The Executive Committee has only three members: a president, a treasurer, and a secretary-general. Interestingly enough, "Pepe" Figueres, has served as the president of his political party since its inception in 1951.

The secretary-general usually serves at the good grace of the PLN's presidential candidate or, if the party has elected one, the chief executive of Costa Rica. He coordinates the work of all party organs, approves new members, both on the national and local level, and coordinates the activities of party members in the National Legislative Assembly, semiautonomous institutions, and other government organizations.

Summary. The PLN is a highly institutionalized organization and, in comparison to other Costa Rican political parties, is characterized by significantly more party discipline and spirit. The other two principal parties have learned that if they do not unite and organize themselves they run the risk of permitting the Figueres organization to retain permanent hegemony in the political arena.

PARTY OF NATIONAL UNIFICATION

The Party of National Unification is made up of the two arch rivals of the 1948 revolution: the *calderonista* National Republican Party (PRN) and the *ulatista* National Union Party (PUN), the leaders of which realized that in order to survive and campaign against the *liberacionistas* effectively, some sort of coalition was required. It was the PRN, under the leadership of its founder Dr. Rafael Calderón Guardia, which in 1948 attempted to annul the election of PUN leader and founder Otílio Ulate Blanco. This maneuver sparked armed opposition to the *calderonistas* and eventually put the PLN under Figueres into a paramount position in national politics. Figueres launched his revolution in support of Ulate, and the PLN leader saw to it that the latter served a full term in office. However, the *ulatistas*, mostly traditionalist members of the prestige social sectors, soon split with the upwardly mobile white-collar groups led by Figueres.

Of the two parties making up National Unification, the PRN is by far the larger of the two groups both in membership and in voter support. After its ouster this organization was capable even of mustering international support, notably that of General Anastasio Somoza, president of Nicaragua, who allowed the PRN to form an armed invasion into Costa Rican territory in 1955. Although strictly a personalist organization, the PRN does retain a sizeable following.

The *calderonistas* have never evinced any sort of integrated ideology, although during the period of coalition with *Vanguardia Popular*, roughly 1942–48, they did have much to say in favor of the working class and did make some attempts to permit this group some upward social mobility. The PRN owns no formal organization and usually restricts its efforts for creating some form of party structure to the period just before an election. Six months before an election a party headquarters is opened in the capital city, with branches in several provincial cities including Limón. Immediately after the election, whether or not victory is attained, the entire party apparatus disappears. Meetings of the party leadership are held in its caucus room at the National Assembly or more than likely in the boardroom of one of the notables' law office. In general the PRN has always been pretty much under the control of a group with a close relationship to former president Calderón. It remains to be seen what happens to this party after its leader expires.

The PUN, which is the other segment of the Unification Party, is even more personalist oriented than the PRN if this is possible. Its organizational pattern is very similar to that of the *calderonistas*; during the campaign period every four years some form of party structure does appear. The followers of Otílio Ulate have never eschewed an ideology. Some idea of where the personalities of the party stand on issues affecting Costa Rica can be obtained when it is realized that the majority of them support the ultra-right wing ANFE interest group. As in the case of the PRN, it remains to be seen what will happen to the PUN after the demise of Ulate.

In the 1966–70 period the Party of National Unification was able to maintain considerable discipline in the National Assembly despite the inevitable differences which must arise in a coalition such as the one between PRN and PUN. One of the deputies was informally chosen as Unification leader; he coordinated the two segments during legislative sessions. Although Unification Party discipline has been able to stand the test of rigorous opposition and debate, it is not comparable to the discipline of the PLN.

Leaders of both PUN and PRN have asserted publicly that they regard the Unification Party as a permanent arrangement, and all past differences have been buried in the interests of gains in the political arena. However, the 1970 election revealed a split between the members of the PRN on this issue. A group of *calderonistas* remains loyal to Unification and supported coalition candidate Mario Echandi during the campaign. Echandi traces his origins to the *ulatistas* rather than to the PRN. However, a small number of PRN notables broke away from the coalition and supported the candidacy of 1966–70 vice-president Virgilio Calvo for the office of chief executive. The reason for the split seems to revolve around the tendency of Unification leaders to avoid running *calderonista* leaders as their candidates or fear of reviving old enmities and to avoid having to argue the issues of the 1948 conflagration once again. Younger members of the PRN, aware that this policy restricts their access to major political patronage positions, apparently balked when Echandi once again became the Unification candidate.

There are undoubtedly other more obscure and personalistic reasons for the split.

SPLINTER GROUPS

Unión Cívica Revolucionaria. Unión Cívica is the only party, other than the PLN and National Unification, which achieved representation in the 1966–70 National Assembly. Led by former Figueres supporter Frank Marshall Jiménez, the *Unión Cívica* won two seats in the National Assembly in that period. Marshall himself assumed one of the seats. He is one of the more colorful of Costa Rica's political activists; at one time he maintained and operated a small army, which made him particularly useful to Figueres during the 1948 hostilities. The army has now degenerated into a small group of loosely organized adventurers and does not compare in organization or firepower with Costa Rica's other private army run by the anticommunist MCRL.

In early 1968 Marshall allowed himself to be imprisoned briefly for dealing in contraband liquor imported from Panama. He waived his immunity as a member of the National Assembly, apparently to elicit the sympathies of his peers.

The *Unión Cívica* apparently was formed after Marshall found it impossible to buckle under to the discipline which quickly became the hallmark of the *liberacionista* party. Because the PLN has maintained only a one-vote majority in the National Assembly since 1958, the *Unión Cívica* when it has achieved representation has wielded more influence than its size would ordinarily merit. Marshall's organization has no ideology and no organizational strength aside from its small paramilitary force and appears to have thrived largely on the popularity, now waning, of its leader.

Partido Revolucionario Auténtico (PRA). Unification 1970 presidential candidate Mario Echandi became disenchanted with the coalition after serving as chief executive from 1958 to 1962 and led a small group in a breakaway just after leaving the presidency. Among the disgruntled notables who joined with Echandi was a former deputy, José Aguilar Bulgarelli. Despite the fact that Echandi has now been reconciled with Unification, the splinter group which he formed continues under the leadership of Aguilar. The organization is much less moderate than when Echandi was involved with it; possibly for this reason the *Partido Revolucionario Auténtico* (PRA) has never won an election.

The party does hold regular meetings and publishes a newspaper which at times does present a perceptive analysis of certain aspects of the national political situation. Mostly the paper and the party are manifestations of Aguilar's personality. For the time being, the PRA serves mainly as a collective gadfly to the large parties and the government of Costa Rica.

Partido Acción Socialista. This organization manifests a number of the old *Vanguardia Popular* labor union people among its leaders. However, to call the *Partido Acción Socialista* a communist party would be inaccurate, since the organization does advocate a program which is highly nationalistic and distinct from the one still promoted by some of the old *Vanguardia* leaders. The *Partido Acción Socialista* operates within the well-defined political arena so highly influenced by the PLN, and it would seem that it is as committed to preserving this system as are any of the other parties. This organization did elect one deputy to the National Assembly in 1962, but until 1970 had not presented a presidential candidate.

The membership of the *Partido Acción Socialista* is small, and its influence in the Costa Rican political decision-making process matches its size. One tactic that it did find useful prior to the 1970 election was to announce which presidential candidate it intended to support during each campaign.

In the 1966 election this group endorsed the candidacy of PLN presidential candidate Daniel Oduber, in a move which could be interpreted as being a kiss of death for the politician. The conservative newspaper, *La Nación*, seized this endorsement as ample evidence of the fact that Oduber was not only of the left wing of his party but was also highly subversive. The *La Nación* campaign against Oduber was so strong that the PLN candidate was eventually able to sue, winning a case of libel against the newspaper.

This party or its associates also publish a weekly newspaper which adheres fairly strictly to the non-Maoist communist line and which is read by approximately five thousand persons weekly. The MCRL, the anticommunist interest group of Costa Rica, has to look far to find one of its enemies.

Christian Democrats. The Christian Democrats remained untried at the polls of Costa Rica through the elections of 1966. In 1970 candidates for several offices including the presidency were presented, the slate receiving only a small percentage of the total vote cast. It is too early to tell whether the party is only a personalist organization surrounding the person of presidential candidate Jorge Monge or if during the 1970s it will become a broader-based group.

The Electoral System

As a result of the 1948 revolution and the attempt by the *calderonistas* to introduce a form of *continuismo* into Costa Rican politics, still another institution with autonomy was introduced by the PLN into the machinery of government. The *liberacionistas* and their allies in 1949 founded the Supreme Tribunal of Elections (TSE) to insure that future elections would be honestly and efficiently administered. The TSE is composed of three members elected by the Supreme Court, each of which serves a six-year term. The terms served by the TSE magistrates are staggered to avoid the possibility of the organizations' adopting one particular type of political preference; they enjoy the same status and immunities which are allotted to Costa Rican Supreme Court justices.

The TSE not only supervises the conduct of elections but also exercises exclusive jurisdiction over the interpretation of those constitutional provisions involving voting, party conduct, and elections in general. The Supreme Court does not become involved in interpreting these issues. The TSE, which operates the year around as a full-fledged government agency, also is responsible for supervising the national civil register. The reason that it has been assigned the task of registering births, deaths, acquisitions of citizenship, and marriages is because this information is needed for the compilation of voting lists. Since these functions have been consolidated under the one institution, fraudulent voting—for many years quite common in Costa Rica—has been curtailed to the point where it is probably negligible.

In addition to interpreting the constitution as it deals with elections, the TSE can veto any legislation of this nature prepared by the National Assembly unless the legislature can muster a two-thirds vote to override the Tribunal. It is assumed that, if the legislators can obtain this much support for a bill in their sharply divided branch of the government, they could probably make the legislation a constitutional amendment if necessary.

Because Costa Rican governments of the pre-1948 period were prone to assume a position of benevolent protectionism over the political party in power at the time of an election, particular care was taken by the founders of the TSE to insure that it would actively intervene to halt any such actions in the future. The TSE serves as a watchdog, blocking any attempts by government officials to campaign from their privileged position for a particular party. This provision includes elected politicians of the executive branch; in 1958 when "Pepe" Figueres attempted to campaign for PLN candidate Francisco Orlich, the TSE publicly reprimanded him for the action.

In 1959, largely at the prompting of the TSE, voting was made compulsory in Costa Rica. Prior to that date registration and voting occurred almost exclusively within the urban areas of the country. In 1958 when approximately one-fifth of the population cast a ballot in the elections of that year, the PLN, dependent on support from rural areas, lost the presidential race. The PLN provided active support for the TSE-suggested legislation; and by 1966, when the *liberacionistas* again lost the presidential race, 85 percent of those eligible to cast a ballot did so.[6] Citizens failing to vote are denied a *cédula*, a form of internal passport, which is needed to perform such simple tasks as cashing a check, receiving delivery of registered mail, or receiving social security benefits.

Perhaps the most powerful weapon in the hands of the TSE is its responsibility for disbursing funds to parties as a reimbursement for their campaign expenditures. As already stated, even the PLN does not depend on its members' contributions financially and could not support its program or organization without the help of the government. Parties are required to submit expense reports to the TSE; this institution then decides, according to the vote received by the political organization, how much it is to receive. It is unusual, however, for a party to receive more funds than it reported spending in a campaign; and, in order for it to receive any financial help at all, it must have received at least 10 percent of the total votes cast in a national election.

Preliminarily, it might be stated that the TSE has had three effects on Costa Rican elections. First, it has definitely insured that

---

[6] Tribunal Suprema de Elecciones, *Computo de votos.*

the country's elections are among the most honest in the world. The entire process is completely out of the hands of the government machinery and is definitely independent of political party control. *Continuismo* and other problems which have plagued certain Latin American countries have been avoided in Costa Rica. Second, the TSE has assured that since the Tribunal was founded in 1949, without exception the chief executive's office has changed hands at each election. This has been one more check on the performance and the abilities of the presidency. And lastly it has, by the methods it uses to disburse campaign funds, assured the longevity of the three principal political parties of Costa Rica and made economic survival a desperate battle on the part of the very small parties.

Working in the favor of the smaller parties like the Christian Democrats and *Unión Cívica* or any organization hitherto unformed is the fact that anyone may register a new political party merely by obtaining twenty-five signatures on a petition to the TSE. This alone is sufficient to obtain a place on the ballot, although the TSE usually also requests a formal statement of party ideology, a list of party statutes, and other information; the party may be banned from participation if it is deemed subversive by the Tribunal.

PROPORTIONAL REPRESENTATION

Maurice Duverger, in his now classic analysis of political parties, states that proportional representation tends to lead to a proliferation of parties in a system.[7] Despite the existence of proportional representation in Costa Rica as a method for electing deputies to the National Assembly, a series of factors work against the proliferation of parties. One of the factors has already been mentioned: the method by which the TSE disburses campaign funds. Another factor is the need for the winning presidential candidate to obtain at least 40 percent of the votes cast in the race for the chief executive's office. The race for the presidency is the key contest every four years; and, unless a party has resigned itself to relative anonymity and no potential growth, merely the occasional capture of one or two seats in the Assembly, it must enter it.

[7] Maurice Duverger, *Political Parties*, rev. ed. (London: Methuen & Co., Ltd., 1961).

Prior to each election the TSE allocates the fifty-seven seats of the National Assembly among Costa Rica's seven provinces according to their latest population figures. Each of the provinces then becomes a multimember district. After the voting has taken place, an electoral quotient is determined by the Tribunal; the seats are divided between the parties accordingly.

The present system—each province rather than the country as a whole being regarded as a multimember district—has tended to permit the PLN to be overrepresented in the National Assembly. Since the 1958 election the *liberacionistas* have consistently received less than 50 percent of the total votes cast in legislative races and yet have maintained an absolute majority in the National Assembly. The absolute majority has been retained by a margin of only one vote, but nevertheless an absolute majority it is. The reason for this favoritism to the PLN is that four of the seven provinces or multi-member districts have boundaries which stretch from the more highly urbanized central plateau areas down to the coasts or to the nation's borders. The provincial multimember districts of Heredia, Cártago, Alajuela, and San José contain large groups of rural residents to offset the votes of their urban capital cities, a factor which has helped the PLN in several electoral races.

Despite its absolute majority of one seat in the National Assembly since 1958 and a larger majority in the 1953–58 period, reasonably strong party discipline, and a coherent program for Costa Rica, the PLN has not taken advantage of the benefits accrued to it by the electoral system. For one thing, the office of chief executive has been in the hands of the opposition 50 percent of the time. And at the same time the legislature experiences an elaborate set of checks on its power, checks which were designed in the main by the PLN during the writing of the 1949 Constitution.

Voting Behavior

As noted in chapter 1, Costa Rica is presently only about 34 percent urban and, as a result, the rural areas of the country are particularly important to political parties attempting to gain elected office. Through the late 1960s, largely because of the image of "Pepe" Figueres, who has assumed national hero proportions of fame within his own lifetime, the PLN has been able to retain the loyalty of over 50 percent of the residents of rural areas, the *minifundistas*, the medium-sized farmers, and the townsfolk. But this majority is gradually being chipped away by the other parties, at the same time that the PLN is becoming increasingly urban and white-collar oriented. In the 1970 election the PLN was still able to retain its image as the party of the *campesino* or peasant.

After elections are announced officially by the TSE in the month of August preceding an election year, campaigning, which has been conducted rather mutedly up to that time, comes out into the open. The first official day of the campaign usually sees the leader of each party aiming political broadsides at the other in the press or in a key speech. While urban residents are treated during the August to February campaign period to parades, trucks with loudspeakers, assemblies, speeches, and newspaper and radio advertisements, as well as walls literally buried under thousands of campaign posters, the inhabitants of the rural regions receive an additional kind of treatment. Villages that in many cases have not seen a politician for four years and that contain perhaps only one government official, a policeman, are usually invaded by caravans of vote seekers during the campaign. Each caravan consists minimally of one leading political figure, a marimba band, a truck bearing posters and leaflets, and, most essentially, copious quantities of beer and *guaro*, the national form of what is known in rural regions of the southern United States as "white lightning." At times a tent is erected; villagers are invited to it to meet the politician, to tell him of their needs, and to drink with him. Promises are made, a splendid time is had by one and all, and then the caravan pulls out of the village on Sunday evening, not to return for another four years. A caravan of this type held on a Sunday requires virtually no advance work, since everyone in the immediate region gathers in the center on that particular day.

PLN militants and leaders have accumulated a wealth of experience in promoting this kind of affair, and the *liberacionistas* have made an attempt to visit every corner of the country during each campaign. Since it is the only party which has consistently presented a full slate of candidates to the voters, their efforts in this regard are not surprising. The Unification Party, lacking any permanent organizational structure, has not been capable of putting on as good a campaign show as has the PLN.

Table 8 provides an overview of Costa Rican voting behavior in four recent national campaigns. Revealed in the table, and of great importance to this analysis, is the rapid rise of voter participation. The number of Costa Ricans casting a ballot in national elections increased by approximately 115 percent in thirteen years, a growth rate which even the country's burgeoning population could not emulate. Because a wide variety of parties have campaigned against the PLN during these elections, figures have simply been listed as PLN or anti-PLN in the Table.

Table 8
COSTA RICAN VOTING BEHAVIOR:
AN OVERVIEW

	1953 Presidential Vote	1953 Legislative Vote
PLN	123,444	114,043
Anti-PLN	67,324	49,391
Total	190,768	163,434
	1958 Presidential Vote	1958 Legislative Vote
PLN	94,788	86,081
Anti-PLN	126,761	110,610
Total	221,549	196,691
	1962 Presidential Vote	1962 Legislative Vote
PLN	192,850	184,135
Anti-PLN	187,273	185,526
Total	380,123	369,661
	1966 Presidential Vote	1966 Legislative Vote
PLN	218,590	202,891
Anti-PLN	222,810	178,905
Total	441,400	381,796

SOURCES: Latin American Data Bank, University of Florida, Gainesville; Tribunal Supremo de Elecciones, *Computo de votos*; and *Costa Rica Election Factbook, 1966.*

While voting in elections has increased rapidly largely because it became compulsory in 1959, voting for the PLN has been dropping proportionately. The number of persons voting for the PLN has increased by less than 95 percent in the thirteen-year period, 20 percent lower than the overall voting figure. While the Figueres organization won landslide victories in every race it entered in the 1953 election, by 1966 it was apparent that the PLN experiences a great deal of difficulty in presidential races where the opposition is united, while it barely maintains a majority with the aid of proportional representation in similar legislative races. Some of the reasons behind this trend away from the PLN are not difficult to fathom. For one thing with the Costa Rican population doubling every twenty years or less, approximately half of the population can no longer remember the glorious revolution of 1948. But much more important is the fact that while voting is almost universal in the more urban areas it has not grown as quickly in the rural areas where the PLN for so long maintained hegemony. Although PLN performance in the cities has improved with each election since 1958, it has been insufficient to gain a majority of the votes in the important and populous cities of San José, Alajuela, Heredia, and Limón. The smaller cities of Puntarenas, Cártago, and Liberia have usually given the *liberacionistas* a majority of their votes.

VOTING BY PROVINCE

There are other patterns to be found in the support which the various Costa Rican political parties receive. Differences in the nature of the provincial multimember districts have resulted in differences in voting behavior. Table 9 provides election data for four presidential races by province. Since 1953 was the exceptional election, the one which took place after the revolution, trends cannot be extracted from data for that year.

As can be seen, Alajuela province gave a majority of its votes to PLN candidates in all but the election of 1966. After the sharp drop in support experienced in 1958, small gains were made in the following election, and then by 1966 the percentage received by the *liberacionistas* slipped under the 50 percent mark. Although Alajuela is still primarily a rural province—approximately 20 percent of all Costa Rican agricultural workers live there—the situation is changing rapidly. By the early 1960s the capital of the province had virtually become a suburb of San José, and the capital city's international airport is located on the outskirts of the city of Alajuela. Also by the early 1960s approximately 20 percent of all Costa Rican industrial workers resided and worked in this province, and others commuted to jobs in San José. This urban growth and the rapidly swelling ranks of the blue-collar workers have been sufficiently important to chip away at the PLN's strength in Alajuela.

The province of Cártago has supported PLN presidential candidates in every election except the one of 1958. In that particular year the split in the party led by Jorge Rossi led to a loss of the

Table 9
PROVINCIAL VOTING DATA:
COSTA RICAN PRESIDENTIAL ELECTIONS

	1953			1958		
	PLN	PLN Per-centage	Anti-PLN	PLN	PLN Per-centage	Anti-PLN
Alajuela	24,623	68%	11,692	21,381	51%	20,750
Cártago	17,724	74	5,904	10,610	40	15,579
Heredia	8,811	62	5,288	7,204	44	8,913
Guanacaste	9,530	58	6,925	9,400	46	10,727
Puntarenas	8,407	58	5,991	6,906	39	10,704
Limón	3,697	54	3,098	3,396	39	5,335
San José	50,652	64	28,426	35,831	39	54,755
	1962			1966		
	PLN	PLN Per-centage	Anti-PLN	PLN	PLN Per-centage	Anti-PLN
Alajuela	36,821	52	33,773	40,059	48	41,835
Cártago	26,764	57	20,224	26,532	51	25,049
Heredia	13,524	48	14,554	16,167	48	16,950
Guanacaste	17,962	54	14,899	21,801	52	20,156
Puntarenas	13,756	45	16,927	17,160	45	21,602
Limón	7,060	33	13,861	7,485	45	9,034
San José	77,222	49	78,729	89,386	53	88,184

SOURCES: Latin American Data Bank, University of Florida at Gainesville; Tribunal Suprema de Elecciones, *Computo de votos.*

province to the opposition. Cártago is almost exclusively an agricultural, coffee-growing area, although recent years have seen the introduction of some light industry. The PLN has been able to retain its dominance in this province, although it experienced a sharp drop in support from 1962 to 1966. During this period Irazu volcano, located in Cártago, erupted, spewing volcanic ash throughout the province, dislocating farmers, and hampering day-by-day living. The ash continued to drift across the province for over a year. The administration of PLN President Francisco Orlich was blamed by many *cartaguenses* for not doing more for their province during this disaster, and their sentiments were reflected in the manner that they voted.

The province of Heredia shares many of the characteristics of Alajuela; its provincial capital has become a suburb of San José;

there are more industrial workers than agricultural workers, while a great number of people travel into the national capital to jobs in offices, factories, shops, and homes. The PLN, with its rural orientation, has been unable to win a majority in this province since 1953; and, until the party devises a formula for gaining the support of more of the urban masses, it appears that it will not be able to change its relative political position in Heredia.

The province of Guanacaste, which is considered to be somewhat of a frontier by the Costa Ricans, contains a work force employed almost exclusively in agriculture. Cattle and sugar are the main products of the province, which is located along the border of Nicaragua. Guanacaste is one of the provinces with no land area in the privileged central plateau area. One very poorly constructed and almost impassable road—the Pan American Highway—links Guanacaste with the capital city. The data in Table 9 reveal that except for the year that the PLN suffered a split in its ranks, 1958, the party has retained its hegemony in very rural Guanacaste. It is reasonably safe to predict that this situation will remain unchanged in the future.

The provinces of Puntarenas and Limón, both of which have almost exclusively agricultural economies, are the exception to the general rule that the PLN receives more support from Costa Rica's rural inhabitants than from urbanites. These two provinces are located on the damp tropical coastlands of the country; it is in these areas where all of the foreign-owned banana plantations are located. When the United Fruit Company originally located in Costa Rica, it established its plantations on the Atlantic coast in Limón province. However, just before World War II the banana plants suffered an onslaught of the so-called "Panama disease," and most of the plantations were closed; new ones were established on the Pacific coast in the province of Puntarenas. For many years the only crop produced on the Atlantic coast was cacao, which is not a very lucrative farming endeavor. By the late 1960s a new breed of bananas had been developed with immunity to the "Panama disease," and cultivation has been resumed in the province of Limón.

A notable percentage of the banana workers on both coasts are of West Indian descent, and until recently these people felt alienated from the mainstream of Costa Rican sociopolitical life. The wave of apathy which swept through Limón in 1966, the drop in voter participation, is one symptom of the continued alienation of the banana workers. In the 1930s it was this banana worker who became the principal target for union organizers of what was to be called the *Vanguardia Popular* movement. Capitalizing on the worldwide depression, the lack of work in the Limón area as the result of the "Panama disease" devastation, plus the generally poor living and working conditions which are normal to these areas, the union men were able to focus the anger of the workers toward "Mamita Yunai," as the United Fruit is popularly known in Costa Rica. A strike in 1937 was crushed by the period's conservative government, which rushed troops down from the central plateau area on the single British-owned railway track that is still the principal method of transportation in Limón.

When *Vanguardia* lent its support to the *calderonistas* in the 1940s, labor in Puntarenas and Limón provinces followed suit, as voting returns for the period reveal. The *calderonistas* have not forgotten this support and have capitalized on it in each election they have participated in since being ousted in 1948. In 1953 the followers of Calderón were not permitted to participate in the elections, and this partially explains the victory of the PLN in the two agricultural and coastal provinces in that year.

Election trends in the province of San José are more difficult to analyze and to explain. Over half of the industrial workers of Costa Rica reside in this province, and yet one-fifth of the entire agricultural labor force also live there. San José province is the most urbanized in the country, but it still depends to a considerable degree on agriculture for the employment of its work force. The *liberacionistas* swept San José in the 1953 election, just as they did every other province in the country. The split in party ranks, which hurt the PLN in 1958 in many areas of the country, accounted for a devastating defeat in San José. By the late 1950s the PLN program was having its effect on this province, where 70 percent of all government workers reside and work. Although the PLN received the support of service sector employees and the agricultural workers of San José province in the 1962 election, this support was insufficient to carry the province. However, by 1966 the government bureaucracy had grown sufficiently to give the PLN a majority, although the Figueres organization did not achieve victory in the capital city itself.

VOTING BY OCCUPATION

No thorough empirical study of Costa Rican voting behavior
has yet been attempted. The analysis which follows is based on educated guesswork rather than on data gathered in the field in any
systematic fashion. Graph 3 represents an attempt to distinguish

Graph 3

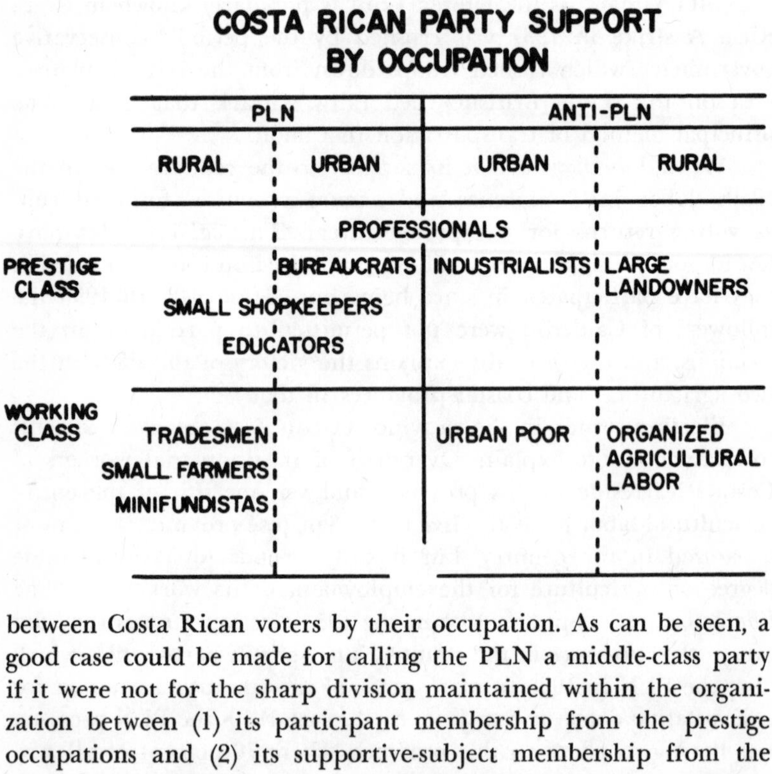

COSTA RICAN PARTY SUPPORT
BY OCCUPATION

	PLN		ANTI-PLN	
	RURAL	URBAN	URBAN	RURAL
PRESTIGE CLASS		PROFESSIONALS BUREAUCRATS SMALL SHOPKEEPERS EDUCATORS	INDUSTRIALISTS	LARGE LANDOWNERS
WORKING CLASS	TRADESMEN SMALL FARMERS MINIFUNDISTAS		URBAN POOR	ORGANIZED AGRICULTURAL LABOR

between Costa Rican voters by their occupation. As can be seen, a
good case could be made for calling the PLN a middle-class party
if it were not for the sharp division maintained within the organization between (1) its participant membership from the prestige
occupations and (2) its supportive-subject membership from the
working class. The prestige-class membership, rather than attempting to weld the party together with a middle-class consciousness and
ideology, appears instead to aspire to acceptance within the national
oligarchy, using the lower-class membership as a springboard with
which to vault themselves upwardly mobile.

During the 1970 election it appears that the PLN made some
inroads into organized agricultural labor in the provinces of
Puntarenas and Limón and gained the support of a larger group

of the urban poor than usual. Whether 1970 was actually a crisis-type election, in which major shifts in party were experienced on all sides, is still difficult to ascertain.

After the 1948 revolution the great majority of Costa Rican professionals supported and voted for the PLN. Those who are employed by the bureaucracy, an ever-growing number, continue to vote for the *liberacionista* organization. In one study of the political attitudes of bureaucrats, 50 percent of those questioned were willing to acknowledge openly their support for the PLN, while only 6 percent acknowledged support of one of the opposition parties.[8] It can be safely suggested that, of the 44 percent who were not willing to declare a party allegiance, there were at least some who regularly voted for and supported the PLN. The majority of bureaucrats do support the Figueres organization; and, as long as the PLN continues to expand the bureaucracy and provide more employment for this group, there is no reason to suspect that they will go over to the opposition. More independent professionals such as lawyers, journalists, and administrators of large private enterprises tend now to split on their party loyalties. Educators as a group vote for the PLN, and their interest group, the ANDE, usually endorses the *liberacionista* slate of candidates.

OTHER FACTORS

There are undoubtedly many other factors which determine the manner in which Costa Ricans vote. Education, the key to upward social mobility, is no doubt an important determinant. Preliminarily it can be hypothesized that Costa Ricans with a university education tend more to vote for the PLN than for one of the other parties. For those with less than a university education, it is impossible even to hypothesize about their voting behavior.

There are also some factors which are unimportant in Costa Rican voting behavior. Race, religion, and language are all non-determinants simply because the country is highly homogenous, an unusual state of affairs for a Latin American country.

SUMMARY

Bearing in mind the fact that Costa Rica is essentially a socially bifurcated society, voting behavior and party support are not diffi-

---

[8] Charles F. Denton, "Bureaucracy in an Immobilist Society: The Case of Costa Rica," *Administrative Science Quarterly* (September, 1969).

cult to understand. Using the data in Table 1 as a basis, it first can be asserted that the slowly shrinking group of the population employed in agriculture and fishing—the great majority of which form part of the working class—supports the PLN. Exceptions to this generality are large landowners and organized agricultural labor in the provinces of Limón and Puntarenas. The rapidly growing group of government employees, most of whom live in San José province, also support the *liberacionistas*; in the main this group is of the prestige class. Members of the industrial group, whether of the prestige or the working class, tend to be anti-PLN, as in the case with persons employed in the service sector of the economy. Owners of large commercial establishments are anti-PLN, while small shopkeepers are supporters of the Figueres party.

Costa Ricans who possess the most status resources tend to be anti-PLN. Small shopkeepers, bureaucrats, educators, and certain professionals whose occupation or background has denied them what they consider their modicum of status, turned to the political arena in 1948 to attempt to become socially more upwardly mobile and to obtain more status. An alliance was formed with small farmers and the residents of towns and villages (as opposed to cities), and the PLN achieved success at the polls after first assuring itself participation by means of a violent uprising. This uprising was successful because of a split in the ranks of the oligarchy at the time. As the PLN has achieved success, it has become less concerned with supplying the demands of its working-class membership and instead has concerned itself with distributing status to its prestige-oriented membership. This status is distributed by permitting participation in an elaborately designed, United States-modeled, democratic government. Despite this shift in its basic orientation, the PLN's elaborate ideology and organization have managed to institutionalize much of the party's support, a support which shrinks formally and slowly with each election.

Since 1948 the anti-PLN groups have been forced to participate in a political arena the context of which has been strongly influenced by the Figueres organization. The oligarchy has also been obliged to share some of its status with the leadership of the PLN. The *calderonistas* and *ulatistas* have survived without formal organizational structures by uniting and by retaining the loyalties of many of their earlier supporters such as organized agricultural labor. The Unification group has also capitalized on the disaffection with the PLN on the part of the urban poor. The working classes of the urban areas, whose expectations are greater than the poor of the countryside, at least partially because of the better educational opportunities offered them, have been more likely to make demands on the political system. When these demands are not met or, more likely than not, when they note that there is little or no difference between the responses to their demands made by either the PLN or the anti-PLN decision makers, the working class becomes disaffected. Since decisions are made within a PLN-ordered political framework, it is with that political party that the responsibility is laid for what they regard as their plight.

The following chapter provides a detailed analysis of the sorts of demands and supports placed on political decision makers in Costa Rica and how these demands are met.

5
The Political Process

The analysis which follows views Costa Rican politics as a process involving the authoritative allocation of resources for the society as a whole.[1] The institutions involved in this process, their origins, and the environment of the political arena have already been examined. The entire process is regarded as an interrelated system with specific functions; these are of three varieties—input, conversion, and output.[2] The final portion of the chapter assumes an overview position of Costa Rican society and provides an analysis of the direction in which the political system is headed, if any, and the effects it is having on the social system as a whole.

Input Functions

Several theorists in the area of comparative politics have suggested dividing systemic inputs into two basic categories—demands and supports.[3] Certain political processes involve the placing of

---

[1] Ths definition has been adapted from several sources including Gabriel A. Almond and James S. Coleman (eds.), *The Politics of the Developing Areas* (Princeton: Princeton University Press, 1960); Robert Dahl, *Modern Political Analysis* (Englewood Cliffs: Prentice-Hall, 1964).

[2] The idea of politics as a system was introduced into the area of comparative politics by several analysts, one of the most important of which is David Easton, *The Political System* (New York: Alfred A. Knopf, 1953).

[3] Such as Almond and Powell, *Comparative Politics*, pp. 16–41.

demands on decision makers while others provide support to the overall system.

DEMANDS

Almond and Powell outline a series of demand inputs which are regarded as functional to their systems model, the first of which is the demand for goods and services.[4]

Goods and Services. Members of a system demand certain economic and social resources from their political system. This particular type of demand closely reflects the bifurcated social structure of Costa Rica in the system under study here

The demand for economic and social resources from the political system is growing steadily in Costa Rica, and in this respect this society is similar to those of other countries in the world. Even countries with an abundance of resources, relatively speaking, are increasingly allocating them through the political process; and fulfilled demands apparently create new ones. In a country with much more limited resources, such as Costa Rica, the creation of new demands must be controlled, or it is probable that the system would quickly disintegrate. However, the control of demands is more aptly termed an output function of the system and will be examined further below.

There are a number of reasons for the growing number of demands for resources made to the Costa Rican political system. A primary one is the slowly narrowing communications gap between the people of the country, a process which makes Costa Ricans aware that certain kinds of resources are available and are being allocated to certain of their countrymen. The nation's homogenous population, its relatively high literacy rate, and its small size geographically insure that this sort of information will eventually become thoroughly disseminated. A second reason for this rise in demands for economic and social resources is that the private sector either could nor or would not provide them, causing the people to turn to their political system for relief. A third reason for this growth is the one outlined above: as demands have been met, new ones have been created.

The rising number of demands placed on Costa Rican decision makers during World War II, particularly those originating with

4 Ibid.

white-collar groups at the lower reaches of the prestige class, created tensions in the political system. No structure in the system being capable of converting these demands, eventually the changes of the 1948 revolution occurred, and the system was adapted to handle them. The formula of the leaders of the 1948 revolution for solving this problem was to be democratic. That is, people would be allowed to organize freely and to bring their grievances to the attention of the government policymakers. The new system has been capable of meeting many of the demands originating with the prestige class by co-opting its members, regulating the growth of the group and, in the final resort, supplying their needs. The same cannot be said for the working class, which has generally experienced more regulation than in the pre-1948 period though fewer of its demands have been met.

The Costa Rican prestige class requests many more social resources from the political system than does the working class. Education, concerts, participation, and, most importantly, status are just a few of this type of demand made by the prestige class and met by the system. Higher education is limited, but this is because resources for maintaining the school system are scarce, as are status positions for graduates. Concerts, which are just one example of a particular type of social resource, are subsidized by the national government. The National Orchestra of Costa Rica is paid by government allocations; and the National Theatre, an exact replica of the Paris Opera House on a smaller scale, is used for all concerts. The price of admission to the concerts and to other events held at the National Theatre is well beyond the means of the working class.

Participation in the political decision-making process is easily obtainable for a well-educated member of Costa Rica's prestige class. The wide variety of interest groups, the country's many newspapers, the active if not always well-organized political parties are always seeking new recruits who are capable of articulating their interests. Status in the prestige class, with its democratic norms, is most easily obtainable by active participation in politics in the case of its male members. For the majority of Costa Rican working-class members, participation is restricted almost exclusively to the formal act of voting. Only once in the country's history has a prestige-class group found it necessary to solicit the support of working-class groups to gain a position in the political arena. The result was a disruption of the system. Since the PLN is now securely entrenched in the system, it no longer needs the support of the working-class groups. The working class makes no demands for status and receives none.

The prestige class also makes demands for certain kinds of scarce economic resources from the Costa Rican political system. This group demands and receives health and banking facilities, insurance, telephones, refined gasoline, airline service, pensions, white-collar positions in the bureaucracy, and increased salaries for government workers. As the decision makers of Costa Rica, particularly those of the PLN, established the institutions necessary to provide many of the above facilities, they justified their actions as being necessary in order to aid the working class of the country. For example, Costa Rica was one of the first countries in the Western Hemisphere to nationalize and expropriate its banking system. The idea behind this move, according to "Pepe" Figueres, who initiated the action, was to make capital more easily available to farmers and members of the working class. Loans would be made using social criteria related to the development of the country rather than to profit making. Each year a few widely publicized operations of this type are carried out; but generally today, just as in other countries, a certain amount of status and economic resources are required as a precondition for a loan. Since the working class has few of these, there is little chance that they could take advantage of the nationalized banking facilities. Even in the simple matter of opening and maintaining a checking account, the working class is excluded. In order to open any kind of a checking account in any of Costa Rica's banks, all of them owned by the state, it is necessary to make a preliminary deposit of three hundred dollars. In a country with a per capita income of four hundred dollars, there are few who can take advantage of this facility.

The banks and other resource-providing institutions do provide scarce jobs to members of the white-collar class, thereby supplying their greatest need—access to economic resources. And since it is members of the white-collar groups who staff the institutions designed to meet demands, present or latent, of the working class, it is not long before their thinking pervades the institutions. Informal criteria for meeting demands are established, and the working class soon finds itself further excluded from the resources it so badly needs, but which are scarce in the society.

Members of the working class make few demands for social resources. Children are expected to feed themselves just as soon as they are able, and education is regarded as of little importance. The long-run rewards are unforeseeable by most members of this group. Demands are made for health facilities by members of the working class, particularly since sickness is more common to their lives than to those of the prestige class. Sports facilities are demanded by and provided for the working class. Soccer football is of particular importance as a sport in the Central American area, witness the so-called "soccer war" of 1969; Costa Rica is no exception. Betting on the football games, which is legal, actually is heavier than purchases of lottery tickets in the country under study here. In a humorous vein, perhaps, it might be suggested that if the government were to close the soccer stadium, then the working class would bring the system down within one week.

In general, working-class people, as contrasted to those of the prestige class, seek those resources which will permit them to get ahead within their social sector. In the case of the working class, it was noted that economic goods and services are all-important for attaining vertical social mobility. Workers on a small scale—and largely as the result of a feedback process—are demanding land, housing, inexpensive food, blue-collar positions, and summer camps. However, since status is required to manipulate the political decision-making process and the working class do not seek, much less have, status, their demands are generally not being met.

In the final analysis, then, each class demands from the polity that type of resource needed to get ahead within its sector of society. Members of the prestige class are primarily demanding status resources or economic resources such as telephones or jet airline service, which in themselves connote status. Since participation in the system itself is status, members of the prestige class eagerly seek a role in the polity. Members of the working class demand economic resources, but because they lack status are not able to manipulate their system adequately. Status politics would be the best way to describe the process in Costa Rica.[5]

Regulation of Behavior. Demands for the regulation of behavior in Costa Rica, the second type of demand outlined by Almond and Powell for their systems model, have been limited since

___

[5] James L. Payne, *Patterns of Conflict in Colombia* (New Haven: Yale University Press, 1968) is the analysis of one Latin American country based on the principle that status is one of the most important reasons for political participation in that country.

the events leading up to the violence in 1948.[6] The white-collar prestige groups, who had their shops and enterprises sacked by the army during the lockout of 1947, were able to gain sufficient status to bring about the virtual elimination of the military.

The reaction against the military remains so strong that in the 1960s, when because of a rising crime rate there was a demand for more protection of private citizens, this type of demand was directed away from the political system. Rather than making demands on the system for increased regulation of behavior, Costa Ricans have organized what are known as *vigilantes* in the neighborhoods inhabited by members of the prestige class. These are private police forces maintained by a small money contribution from each resident monthly. All of the better residential areas of the cities have *vigilante* service. Unfortunately if a resident of a neighborhood decides not to contribute any more to the *vigilante* force, his home is broken into and robbed regularly until he once again changes his mind. In the poor neighborhoods it is not unusual for the residents to get together and pay one of their neighbors a small sum of money to watch their homes each night. *Vigilantes* operate in urban centers throughout the country including Limón, Puntarenas, Cártago, Escazú, Santa Ana, and the San José metropolitan area itself.

Demands for the regulation of behavior which are emitted into the political system usually originate from the prestige class of society and are often meant only to be applied to the working class. The prevailing attitude among the members of the status-oriented class is that the legal system is designed for their benefit and for preventing incursions on their rights by members of the working class. This is often the way justice is meted out also as revealed by statistics on the backgrounds of prisoners at San José's Central Penitentiary in an earlier chapter. Upper-class Costa Ricans have learned from the example of many other Latin American countries that, if they begin to demand more efficient regulation of behavior from their political system, eventually they themselves will be regulated. "Law and order" is not a popular plank in the campaign platform of any of the country's political parties.

Demands for Participation. Participation, a form of status resource, has already been discussed in this chapter and in the previous

[6] Almond and Powell, *Comparative Politics*, pp. 16–41.

one. The social class structure, coupled with several formal and informal political mechanisms such as the electoral system, insures that demands of this type originating with upper social status groups living in the central plateau regions are more likely to be successful than those of other groups. As a result, working-class groups are not demanding or receiving participation from the system. Democratic procedures, such as proportional representation, free elections, and limitations on the power and terms of office of elected officials, have not been sufficient to insure a reasonably equal participation for all in the system.

Symbolic Displays. Almond and Powell outline a fourth kind of demand in their systems model, a demand which they label as symbolic displays.[7] Costa Ricans make few demands of this type on their system, and, as a result, symbolic output takes on a form different from that of other countries. The prestige class have not even been sufficiently nationalistic to initiate a "buy Costa Rican" campaign, perhaps because this would deprive them of their status-connected purchases of imported goods and services. Nationalism, then, is limited in Costa Rica. Joseph Nye states:

It is not accurate to depict Central American states as devoid of nationalistic ideologies . . . a considerable degree of national consciousness exists in most Central American states, but it has not been intensified to a high degree or exclusiveness, by an elite nationalist ideology. In the past this was both because of the low levels of urbanization and the cosmopolitan Europe-oriented nature of the elites. . . Among the nationalist elite today, the reasons for not developing a more intense and exclusive nationalist ideology are attributable partly to the past, but more to the distance from direct colonial experience and to appraisal of the limited political benefits available because of the geographical location.[8]

Nationalism is muted not only in the context of a development ideology but also in terms of loyalty and emotional attachment by the population to the government.[9]

Demands for Change. Not included in the Almond and Powell model but of vital importance to the understanding of the Costa

[7] Ibid.

[8] Nye, "Central American Regional Integration," pp. 30–31.

[9] For an interesting analysis of the role of ideology in developing nations, see Gideon Sjoberg, "Ideology and Social Organization in Rapidly Developing Societies" (Report delivered to the Comparative Administrative Group Conference, University of Maryland, April, 1966).

Rican political process is the source of demands for change, if any, and how these demands are processed. It has already been noted that prior to 1948 in Costa Rica there was a dysfunctional demand on the polity to supply certain types of resources which eventually brought major disruptions in the system and the creation of new institutions; marginal members of the prestige class, which potentially could have become a class in themselves, instead became more thoroughly accepted as members of a single upper class.

Demands for change in the political system were not widespread in the late 1960s whether in reference to the prestige class or to the working class. There is no large, coherent, and alienated group unwilling to work within the context of the system as it exists now. The urban working class is discontent with the PLN but still works within the system, as does the organized group of agricultural laborers. Until members of the prestige class become disaffected and once again look for alliances with members of the working class, demands for change will be few and far between. There are demands from members of the prestige class for incrementalist type changes and mild reforms, but never for radical changes in the general political and socioeconomic processes that might solve some of the more serious of Costa Rica's problems. For example, no one suggests totally eliminating the importation of luxury commodities.

SUPPORTS

A second type of inputs is described by Almond and Powell for their systems model—supports.[10] The support function permits the system to survive and to maintain itself even as demands are made upon it. Perhaps the most important type of support is the one which involves the provision of economic resources to the system. The resources supplied to the system are then used to pay salaries and to allocate among the various groups making demands for them.

Table 10 provides data on the sources of government income in Costa Rica for a single year. As has been pointed out, taxation has generally been of the indirect or nongraduated variety, burdening the individual with a lower income more than the prosperous person. Income taxes in Costa Rica rank third as provider of economic resources to the political system. Although sales taxes are

[10] Almond and Powell, *Comparative Politics.*

Table 10

COSTA RICAN GOVERNMENT INCOME SOURCES, 1966

(percentages)

Taxes Levied on Imports	51.57%
Loans from National and International Sources	18.25
Income Taxes	12.90
Property Taxes	3.77
Sales Taxes, revenues for services provided, and other	13.51
Total	100.00%

SOURCE: *Anuario estadístico de Costa Rica, 1966*, p. 270.

not as important as the income tax, when the 5 to 25 percent rate is more thoroughly enforced in the country, it can be expected that sales tax will overtake income tax as a supplier of revenue.

The principal source of government income continues to be duties levied on imports, a situation with important implications. Primary among them is the effect they have on the public administration. It can hardly be expected that bureaucrats would vociferously advocate the curtailment of imports, clearly a necessity considering the long term imbalance of trade faced by Costa Rica, when they depend on these imports for revenues perhaps to pay their very salaries. In addition, of course, the bureaucrats are members of the prestige class who conspicuously consume imported luxury commodities. High import duties in Costa Rica can be regarded from at least two angles then. They can be viewed as an impetus to industrialization as suggested by "Pepe" Figueres of the PLN, or they can be regarded as one method to obtain revenues to support the present political system.

As revealed by the data in Table 10, material supports from within the country have not sufficed to meet the needs of the government; income from the international environment of Costa Rican society is required to finance annual deficits. If regular inflows of economic resources did not occur from abroad, the political system would have to curtail its allocations or restrict demand, either course of action probably causing disruptions in the political process.

The provision of service supports, such as the free or almost gratis labor proffered in other countries, does not exist in Costa Rica. There is no military conscription or corps of volunteers to provide social resources to the political system for limited periods of time. Certain professionals, in exchange for a license to practice or to teach are required to provide one year of service to the government, such as being assigned to certain rural areas to provide badly needed services there. This regulation is honored in the breach, however, which is not surprising, considering that it affects members of the prestige class.

Obedience Supports. Obedience supports are still another of the inputs outlined by Almond and Powell for their systemic model.[11] Obedience to rules and regulations made by a political system result in support inputs. As in the case of other inputs in Costa Rica, the class structure of the society determines the nature of the inputs. The prestige class does not feel as bound to provide this type of support as do the members of the working class, for in their eyes the system is designed to function for the former rather than for the latter. It has already been noted that members of the upper class rarely go to prison in Costa Rica. The average policeman, recruited from the working class by an upper-class politician, is loath to accuse a member of the white-collar group of committing an infraction of any sort. Members of the prestige class know that the rules and regulations they have designed are not applicable to them, but rather to the mass of the people. For example, in an office of the public administration it is common to see the sign "Positively No Admittance," which is designed to prevent the public from entering into certain work areas. Administrators expect members of the prestige social class to ignore such a sign and at the same time refuse to stand in line with the rest of the people. But a "Positively No Admittance" sign in an office of the Costa Rican public administration means that members of the working class must not pass, and there is no exception.

It must be pointed out that the attitude toward rules and regulations displayed by Costa Rican upper-class persons is not malicious and is usually not even conscious. It is rather a pattern of behavior learned from childhood and is expected of this class by persons of the working class. To the tourist this general attitude is evident the minute he embarks on a Costa Rican road. San José motorists, for example, usually upper-class individuals, feel no com-

11 Ibid.

pulsion to heed signals from inanimate objects such as stop signs and directional lights.

The working class, in contrast to their mentors, feel a strong compulsion to obey all rules and regulations. Perhaps the reason for this is that the members of the class have their behavior more regulated than do the prestige-class Costa Ricans. Trained to an authoritarian-submissive attitude, the working-class member obeys unquestioningly all regulations which he is aware of. A good deal of the curriculum in the first grade in the nation's public schools is designed to make him aware of the sort of behavior expected of him. The small amount of education proffered to most working-class Costa Ricans could, in fact, be regarded as still another tension control mechanism for the political system. By politicizing the youngsters at an earlier age than is common in some Latin American countries, the system is assured of continuing obedience for a lifetime.

Symbolic Support. Just as Costa Ricans demand very few symbolic outputs from their system, so also do they provide very few. Political leaders are often referred to by their nicknames, and everyone actually addressed Figueres as Don "Pepe" when he occupied the presidency. National monuments are few and unheeded, as is the national flag.

APATHY

Apathy is an input often neglected by systems analysts in the area of comparative politics. And yet in the Costa Rican political system it is just as important a support as any of the ones already examined. Because of the limited social and economic resources in Costa Rica, decision makers are limited in their ability to convert demands and supports into action. The controlling of demands and the regulating of tensions are not sufficient. It is also necessary for a large group of the population to be apathetic, to ask nothing from their system, and yet to obey its rules and regulations.

The present nature of the Costa Rican political process requires that members of the working class be largely apathetic to it and leave the operation of the system to those who count. On the other hand, apathy can be only limitedly tolerated in members of the prestige class; and, if this sort of attitude were to become widespread, it could be dysfunctional to the system. In order to compensate for the at-times erratic decisions made by an apathetic but enfranchised working class, it is necessary for the maximum number of upper-class Costa Ricans to vote.

Apathy as a function to the system has been one of the most delicate problems faced by the PLN. In order for the *liberacionistas* to win an election, it is necessary to insure that a maximum percentage of the population casts a ballot. Since the PLN depends on rural support—where participation is lowest—to gain elected office for its leaders, it must encourage the entire population to vote, even to making the casting of a ballot compulsory if necessary. And yet, if members of the working class are encouraged too greatly, the result may be an increase in the demands placed on the system, rising expectations, and eventual disenchantment. This has begun to occur among members of the urban working class. Apathetic people with little information are compelled to vote, resulting in erratic and unpredictable decisions by the voter. Personalism becomes more important than anything else in this type of a situation.

Apathy is primarily encouraged through a feedback process; members of the working class have learned that despite declarations to the contrary their system will do very little for them. Unless some form of prestige-class leadership is provided to this group, apathy will continue to be the most common characteristic of the citizens of Costa Rica.

Conversion

The institutions charged with converting the demands and supports placed on the Costa Rican political system have already been examined. It remains now briefly to look at the method in which these institutions process the inputs made to them.

Given Costa Rica's relatively high literacy rate, its homogenous population, and its small size geographically—three factors which considerably facilitate communication coupled with the country's limited resources—decision makers have been faced with a large number of demands to convert, but with only limited resources to meet the demands. As a result, they have been forced to control or to obliterate certain demands and, if possible, the institutions making them, to produce a great deal of symbolic output which gives the appearance that demands are indeed being met. Despite the relatively great amount of political activity in Costa Rica, the plethora of institutions and declarations by politicians, very few demands placed on the system are actually converted into authoritative rules.

This situation would certainly bring instant dissatisfaction to many if it were not that almost half of the entire prestige class has been given a stake in the present system. Dependent on the massive—for Costa Rica—governmental apparatus for the provision of economic and social resources, members of the prestige class can hardly be expected to attempt radical changes in it. In other words, Costa Rica's political system is capable of maintaining itself despite its limited resources and drastically curtailed capability for action simply by co-opting the most articulate members of the society and employing them. Moreover, the members of the prestige class have shown themselves eager to be co-opted no matter what their political ideology. For example, *Vanguardia Popular* founder and communist leader Manuel Mora Valverde has been quite willing to accept diplomatic appointments from the government. In the late 1960s he spent considerable time behind the Iron Curtain peddling Costa Rican coffee to the Eastern European nations.

Given the small size of Costa Rica and the even smaller size of its prestige class, the most important method by which demands are converted into authoritative decisions is by contact between members of this group. Legislators consider their sojourn in the National Assembly to be an opportunity to establish contacts through the governmental apparatus to be used later either on their own behalf or on behalf of a client from the prestige class or from a foreign country. The simplest way to get something done in Costa Rica, then, is simply to see a friend in the legislature, in the bureaucracy, or in a political party or interest group and to ask him to help you.

When a member of an elite group or the group itself resorts to a second method for attempting to have their demands converted into authoritative decisions on their behalf, their motivations and goals are more difficult to fathom. Letters to the editors of newspapers, advertisements in the press, meetings, and the use of loudspeaker trucks—all designed to shape Costa Rican public opinion in favor of a particular demand—appear to be a highly inefficient method to have a demand converted. The group conducting this type of campaign is not interested in enlisting the help of working-class groups, who rarely count in the decision-making process anyway and for whom some reward would have to be made. In the case of ANFE, the reason for conducting this type of campaign has already been discussed. This organization deliberately diffuses its demands because it does not wish to have them met. ANFE instead attempts to shape the political climate of the country so that, when elite contacts are made, its genuine viewpoint will appear moderate to decision makers.

Another reason for conducting this kind of campaign is if members of a group do not have adequate contacts in the political arena and are attempting to make them. The anticommunist MCRL seeks allies in important decision-making posts and has found that by advertising heavily a great deal of introduction and explanation are not required when elite contacts are made. And finally in the case of demands, where the prestige class is found to be almost evenly divided on whether they should be met, one side or another may attempt to broadside the other into submission by a rapid attack in the press.

Least important of the methods for having a demand converted into authoritative decisions in Costa Rica is the use of demonstrations and violence. Political decision makers have two distinct ways of handling this form of presenting a demand, depending on the social class from which it originates. Since members of the working class do not have elite contacts and rarely have access to public opinion–forming media of communication, demonstrations and possibly violence are the only methods open to them for making their demands heard. Since in the main this class is apathetic, law and order usually prevail in Costa Rica despite the inefficiency of the National Guard. On the occasion when working-class groups have seen fit to band together to demonstrate, decision makers have taken immediate steps to stamp out this sort of thing violently.

The National Water and Aqueducts Authority (SNAA), a semi-autonomous institution of the Costa Rican public administration, attempted to raise the price on water supplied to consumers in 1967. Working-class groups, who were already receiving mediocre service, regarded this as an insufferable action on the part of the government. Prior to the establishment of the SNAA by the PLN, water, albeit unsanitary, had been provided by the cantons free of charge. Unable to see the benefits of the new institute's service, which was charging them for a vital commodity, grumbling people began to gather in lower-class neighborhoods.

A permit for a demonstration was refused an organizing group by the governor of San José province, a political appointee of the national chief executive who can be removed from office at any moment by the president. A decision was made to hold the demonstration anyway; the group ran an advertisement in all national newspapers declaring that it was their constitutional right to assemble. On a sunny Sunday morning in November, 1967, several thousand members of the Costa Rican working class—including men, women, and children—assembled in San José's Central Park. The Governor gave the order, and the National Guard forcibly evicted the group from the park. Because the police are inexpertly trained, a great deal of unnecessary violence was used in breaking up the demonstration. Although by 1968 the price of water had not been raised, it seems inevitable that it eventually will be.

In contrast to the demonstration against water price hikes by members of the working class is the already-mentioned demonstration by university students against a cut in their institution's budget by the National Assembly. Involved in this demonstration were the sons and daughters of the prestige class, and the reception accorded them was different from the one experienced by the working-class group. The students on a September, 1967, morning marched with a police escort from the Rodrigo Facio campus to the legislative palace. Leaders of the National Assembly met a delegation on the steps of the building and promised to take immediate action on their demands. The PLN, some of whose leaders marched in the demonstration, took out advertisements in the newspaper proclaiming the justice of the student demands. The University of Costa Rica budget was not reduced largely because of the demonstration.

The students who marched in the protest parade were members of the prestige class who in the main had not yet been co-opted by the political system. Since the parade occurred on a weekday, students who also worked for a living were at their jobs. As is the case in many Latin American countries, the university student has the most potential for bringing change to the society of Costa Rica. However, the student in this country has not adopted a political stance to the extent that students have in other countries. Only in the case of issues which directly affect him has the student been willing to enter the political arena.

AUTHORITATIVE DECISION MAKING

The large number of institutions engaged in this function, the fact that there is very little coordination between them, the problem which makes them appear to be working at cross-purposes, and the overlapping of responsibility have already been discussed. Even when demands are clearly articulated to decision makers in the political arena through elite contact or some other method, there is no assurance that authoritative decisions will be made. For decision-making power is diffused throughout the system, and, even if a decision is made, there is no assurance that it will be enforced. As has already been discussed, the overall picture of Costa Rican government is *immobilism*.

A brief look at the budget-making process in Costa Rica is presented here to provide one case study of the authoritative decision-making process in the country. Since the budget involves the allocation of scarce economic resources to the society, it is perhaps more significant than many other authoritative decisions made in the system. As mentioned, the budget is currently prepared by a department in the branch of government headed by the chief executive. The Department for the Coordination and Control of Programs in the National Office of Planning is the closest thing to a budget bureau located in the executive branch of the government, and it is with the assistance of this department that the president prepares his budget.

Each department of the public administration, semiautonomous institutions included, theoretically must submit its annual program to this department of the National Office of Planning. There public investments and expenditures are scaled according to the president's assessment of the current political situation and the country's needs. A budget of sorts is prepared, including investment figures, for the entire government. This department, which could be a powerful weapon in the hands of a program-conscious chief executive, is severely limited in its capabilities. First, it cannot force the semiautonomous institutions to submit their needs to it; and many of them do not, preferring to deal directly with the Bureau of the Budget under the jurisdiction of the National Assembly. Second, as part of the effort to keep the office of chief executive weakened, by order of the National Planning Act the Department for the Coordination and Control of Programs employs only two administrators and one clerk. With a staff of this size the capabilities of this department are severely limited.

Heads of the various departments of the public administration, interest groups, and parties do little to attempt to influence the allocation of resources by the budget at the National Office of Planning stage. At the same time the two administrators of the department make few changes in the requirements presented by the various agencies and institutions. One of the administrators does write a regular economic column in the *La Nación* newspaper, but, other than that, there is relatively little interchange between the system and its environment at this point.

When the budget comes over from the executive branch of the government, the National Assembly sends it to the Committee on Budgetary Affairs, where it is examined for approximately one month. At this time the full force of the political arena is felt by the committee members as prestige-class Costa Ricans jockey for the resources and status which can be allocated by the budget. During the time it is in committee the party in opposition does its best to pare down, slice, and eliminate portions of the budget. When the president's party does not have a majority in the National Assembly, as has been the case for eight years out of the 1953–70 period, cuts are particularly drastic. The PLN in the name of "democracy" has felt free to slash portions out of a number of programs which the party itself established while in control of the presidency.

The Committee on Budgetary Affairs holds hearings at which representatives of various agencies and proponents of programs testify. Full press coverage is provided these hearings, and editorials, columns, and advertisements appear pro or con a particular program. While contacts are made informally between members of the elite, some groups find it necessary—and admittedly this is unusual—to organize demonstrations in favor of their activity. The case of the students in 1967 has already been discussed. By the time the budget is reported out to the full Assembly, it has usually been cut back considerably.

Long and acrimonious debate lasting up to several months characterizes the consideration of the budget in Costa Rica. During this time the informal contacts and the petitions, along with the pressures by the mass media of communications, continue. The budget is discussed item by item by the legislators during this period, with many of the deputies in the opposition knowing little more about their arguments than the fact that the budget originated with a party other than their own. After the budget is finally approved, it is sent to the chief executive, who can veto it if he so desires. The president cannot, however, veto items in the budget, but must approve or disapprove the entire package. The latter course of action, although threatened occasionally, is never taken. Once signed by the president, the program is sent to the Bureau of the Budget, where this agency oversees its implementation. It should be remembered that the Bureau of the Budget is a legislative agency, which means that the president does not supervise it.

The end result of this one particularly important annual conversion process is that the budget rarely includes amounts for innovative attempts to solve Costa Rica's problems. When both the president and the majority party in the legislature are of the same party—usually the case when the PLN wins the office of the chief executive—there is a greater possibility for some change. But given the limited resources of the country, great change would require concomitant amounts of dislocation, a price the system has been unwilling to pay. The more established programs of the government experience little difficulty in securing operating revenues at least sufficient to meet their payrolls. However, the funds for the semi-autonomous agencies, charged with bringing change to Costa Rica, are never sufficient to carry out their allotted program. This is because of the peculiar relationship between these agencies of the bureaucracy and the political arena. Although deeply involved in politics, they often experience difficulties in mobilizing their clientele and to carry out their change-oriented goals; much less likely to organize them to bring pressure on political decision makers.

COMMUNICATION

Essential to all human interaction is the ability to communicate. Communication as a political function is input, output, and conversion function of the system. Costa Rica presents a peculiar problem in this area. It is a small, compact, homogenous country where everybody speaks the same language. Physical communication facilities, although neglected, nevertheless exist in most parts of the country. Literacy is relatively high, newspapers circulate widely, and the transistor radio has made it possible to communicate news and information to virtually the entire population. If there is a

Latin American country where communications do not constitute an insuperable problem, Costa Rica is the one.

While many political systems are facing a problem of over-centralization, this is a minor problem in many respects to Costa Rica. It is true that the system is overcentralized on the central plateau, making communication from the rural areas to decision makers particularly difficult. There is no doubt that the 40 percent of the population not resident in the central plateau experiences difficulty in communicating with political decision makers and that the latter have problems in communicating with this segment of the population simply because agencies of the bureaucracy, interest groups, political parties, and even the mass media have no offices in these areas. Inputs to the system are particularly unlikely from this area. Indicative of this state of affairs is the fact that only thirteen (24 percent) of the fifty-seven National Assembly deputies in the 1966–70 legislature maintained a residence away from the central plateau, and in several cases these were farms operated by a manager and visited occasionally by the politician.

Coupled with this geographical centralization hampering the conversion process is the institutional decentralization already discussed. Bottlenecks occur in the Costa Rican government because information and communication is so diffuse that decisions cannot be made without distortions. Each of the semiautonomous institutions, for example, has its own planning department and feels under no compulsion to communicate its programs to other government agencies. Legislative committees lack expert information that would permit them to communicate to other branches of the government or even to their political parties how particular demands are being met. The chief executive is supplied minimal information about the problems and plans of his government because he has a limited staff to receive the data and because there are major communication gaps in the hierarchy.

These severe communication problems hampering the political conversion process are functional to the system, however. Since resources are so very limited, if communication were suddenly to be improved drastically, authoritative decisions would be made in such a manner as to exhaust the capabilities of the system quickly and possibly to bring about its disintegration. Or, if not, authoritative decisions would have to be made limiting the ability of groups in the environment to make demands on the decision makers, even if these groups were of the prestige class of the society. This would radically alter the nature of the system, and it could no longer then be termed as "democratic" by nature. In a bargaining situation it is often helpful to plead misunderstanding or lack of comprehension; the opposite party will continue to attempt to inculcate understanding with the hope that sooner or later it will achieve its goals. This is easily compared to the relationship between political decision makers and their socioeconomic cultural environment in Costa Rica. The tremendous gaps in communication are an excuse for not performing.

Looking at another area of communication, that of the mass media, there is no independent source of information which could fill the gaps in the Costa Rican conversion process. All of the newspapers, radio stations, and television broadcasters favor one group over another in the political arena. The often-mentioned *La Nación* systematically sides with the anti-PLN groups and does not hesitate to distort their political positions favorably while ignoring the PLN. Since this is the most widely read newspaper in the republic— circulation sixty thousand—it has been a major roadblock in PLN activities. *La República* and *La Prensa Libre*, widely read journals but with smaller circulations than *La Nación*, systematically have favored the PLN in their coverage. As radio stations are usually owned by newspapers, the broadcasting situation is little different. The mass media have been unable to fill the communications gaps in the political conversion process resulting from the decentralization of authority. It is almost impossible to attach responsibilities in the system because of this situation.

The 60 percent of Costa Ricans who have not progressed beyond the third grade represent another sort of communications gap. This group, rather than presenting its own needs and opinions to decision makers to be converted into policy, instead must rely on members of the elite for guidance, perhaps even on how to vote. This communications gap has permitted a smaller group to control the decision-making process, and it is clear that the prestige class takes care of its own interests first. A rapid rise in the educational level of all Costa Ricans would have the same disruptive effects that any radical change would have on the country's political system. Low educational levels insure apathy and only limited demands for the even more limited resources available for allocation by the system.

SOCIALIZATION

Like the function of communication, socialization cannot aptly be labeled strictly a conversion function, for it affects both inputs and outputs to the system. Socialization is the process which affects Costa Ricans' perception of their political system, a subject which has already been discussed in some depth. The way that people are socialized in Costa Rica has also been analyzed.

Just as the educational system is the key to vertical social mobility, so also is it the main agent of political socialization. Children at different levels of education and in distinct kinds of schools are politically socialized differently. As mentioned, those who attend only the primary school are taught obedience to the system, without any sense of participation. In the private high schools the situation is different, as one study reveals.[12] Goldrich asked elite Costa Rican high school students, "How interested are you in politics?" Only 13 percent answered "Not at all."[13] And 79 percent of these students mentioned the name of a party when asked, "With what political party are you affiliated?" The children of members of the prestige class are anything but apathetic toward politics; their participation is functional to the system.

Goldrich's is the only empirical analysis conducted of political socialization processes in Costa Rica yet to be available to the discipline. As a result, what follows is based on educated guesswork and participant observation rather than on data gathered in the field. In contrast to many of the Latin American countries, there are few discontinuities in the political socialization process in Costa Rica. In his contacts with the various agents of socialization, his family, the school, his first job, the bureaucracy, his friends, a young member of the prestige class encounters the same values, the same deference from the working class, and the same political attitudes in each. Even his university professors and campus comrades hold to the democratic norms, general social attitudes, and views toward participation of the prestige class. Costa Rica is small enough so that the young member of the prestige class can count on being known everywhere he goes, on obtaining a status job as soon as he is ready for it, and on participating in the programs and campaigns

[12] Goldrich, *Sons of the Establishment.*
[13] Ibid., pp. 103–33.

of the political party of his choice, usually his father's, just as soon as he is ready. In fact, members of the prestige class are recruited into positions of political leadership as soon as they show an active interest in what goes on in the arena.

Like the prestige class, the working class suffers no discontinuities in its exposure to the political culture of Costa Rica. Here there are no maids to anticipate every need; the working-class child learns to obey, to pay deference, and to expect little participation in the affairs around him. At school the rules and regulations are carefully learned by rote, while his first job could be anything from shining shoes to collecting bus fares. Political personalities in some cases, such as "Pepe" Figueres, are followed in much the same way as are the stars of soccer football; but generally the latter are much more important to the working-class Costa Rican. Apathy in the face of a lower station in life and a lack of participation in the "democratic" government is the attitude members of the working class are socialized into. Since there are no discontinuities in either the socialization process experienced by this group or by the members of the prestige class, little wonder that the Costa Rican socioeconomic political system is immobilist. As Costa Ricans are prone to say, "*Aqui se vive tranquilo*" ("Here we live in tranquility"). Considering the problems faced by the country, its scarce resources, its rapidly growing population, one cannot help but wonder if they can afford that much tranquility.

Output Functions

The outputs of the systems model designed by Almond and Powell are related to the inputs according to the effectiveness of the conversion process. The first output to be considered here is labeled by the two analysts as the extraction of economic and social resources from the environment. As has been repeated throughout the book, the Costa Rican political system has shown itself to be particularly adept at employing members of the prestige class, to recruit them into policy-making roles. The extraction of this type of social resource, leadership, has not been difficult.

Data has also been provided in Table 10 to show where the system receives the resources which it allocates. Although this income was then considered as a support input, it can also be considered as an extractive output. There is no doubt that many people in Costa Rica do not enjoy paying taxes, customs duties, and so on; they do so only because the political system will employ sanctions against them if they do not. Members of the prestige class, who feel under no compulsion to pay income taxes, at the behest of the AID international agency are gradually being forced to pay.

As noted, however, the system has tended to extract proportionately more from the lower sectors of the population, converting resources into benefits for the prestige class. Except for subsistence farmers, virtually everyone in Costa Rica must consume imported commodities regularly, paying customs duties on them. These import levies are obligatory, regardless of the ability of an individual to pay. The same can be said for the recently adopted sales tax in Costa Rica.

Also as already discussed, the system of extraction is not totally self-sufficient. The political system must obtain a certain percentage of the resources which it requires from international sources upon which authority cannot be used. If the United States, for example, were to refuse capital, either public or private, to the Costa Rican government, a dysfunction would be quickly created not only in the political system but also in the socioeconomic system of the Central American republic.

ALLOCATIVE OUTPUT

One of the most important things to consider when viewing the political process of a country is how the resources which the system extracts or receives as a support are allocated to the various elements in its environment. Table 11, providing these figures for Costa Rica, includes government ministries as well as the semiautonomous institutions. Not noted in the table is the fact that since 1950 in no year has the percentage of public sector expenditures made by the semiautonomous institutions sunk below 36 percent, and in 1968 the percentage rose to over 50 percent.

Since the Costa Rican political system has been fairly stable since 1958, it is safe to assume that the allocations shown in Table 11 are satisfying those groups capable of making demands and of providing supports to the system. The obvious emphasis on education, with the comparatively low importance given to defense,

Table 11
EXPENSES OF COSTA RICAN GOVERNMENT, 1966
(in percentages)

Item	Percentage
Education	27.07
Transportation and Communication	13.12
Administrative Expenses	15.66
Servicing Internal Debt	11.24
Social Security	7.01
Community Services	3.75
Public Health	5.78
Servicing External Debt	6.42
Defense	3.58
Other	6.37
Total	100.00

SOURCE: *Anuario estadístico de Costa Rica, 1966*, p. 271.

which includes the police, provides some guidance as to the average upper-class Costa Rican's scale of values. It would seem probable, with the heavy emphasis placed on education, that there would be more upward social mobility and certainly a larger pool of technology than there is in the country. But for most Costa Ricans the educational system has been used to politicize rather than to serve as an instrument for change; the emphasis has been on adapting the citizenry to the rather static system in which they are to live out their lives. The lack of technology in relation to investment in education can be attributed to a scale of values that finds certain professions such as business and the sciences to connote less prestige and status than law and the liberal arts, especially philosophy. Members of the prestige class find it demeaning to consider careers such as engineering or accounting, but the Department of Philosophy at the University of Costa Rica has the largest undergraduate enrollment in the institution.

Also significant data in Table 11 is the percentage of the government's expenses which are allocated to administrative expenses. Decision makers are willing to allocate a sizeable percentage of the available resources for maintaining the bureaucratic system, for paying the salaries of the large group of white-collar workers, and for recruiting new leadership to the system. Since a sizeable amount of the percentage allocated to transportation and communications, which largely involves road building and maintenance, is also given over to administrative expenses, perhaps as much as 20 percent of the national government's expenses for maintaining the prestige-class work force.

SYMBOLIC OUTPUT

In a society with a paucity of resources, the symbolic outputs of its political system can be among the most important functions of that system. The environment must be made to believe that every effort is being made to change the situation the country finds itself in. As has been noted, Costa Ricans do not demand nationalistic symbolic outputs from their system; but symbolic outputs they demand nevertheless.

One of the more interesting results of the scarcity of resources in the country, coupled with certain symbolic demands on decision makers, is that Costa Rican tradition calls for government officials, elected and permanent, to go without comfortable quarters, ostentatious surroundings, and other fringe benefits common to officials of similar status in other nations. Frugal living is considered the democratic way for politicians and officials to demonstrate that they are not robbing the people. The president of Costa Rica resides in a dingy building next to the National Liquor Industry's plant; the latter is a government monopoly. Nine months of the year the president and his family are subjected to the distillery's odors; only during the other three months—the dry season—do the winds blow the fumes in another direction, providing temporary respite. Upstairs over the president's quarters is an office building containing the cabinet room, the vice-president's office, and quarters for the National Office of Planning. One group of planners eventually had to be moved out of this building because their walking around on the uncarpeted floors kept the president and his family from getting their rest.

While maintaining the pose of austerity, the political system and its decision makers make great efforts to publicize their accomplishments to the people. The overall effect is to give the impression of a poor, aggressive, and democratic system which does not have time for such things as uniforms, pomp, and other finery because it is too busy bringing great changes to the country, particularly to the working class.

Prospects for Change

The ability of the Costa Rican political system to adapt to its environment requires no further analysis here. As has been repeated almost to the point of redundancy, the political system has shown itself quite capable of converting into outputs the demands and supports fed into it by groups in the prestige class, the only ones capable of voicing demands. System maintenance and adaptation are not at issue here; rather it is of interest to view the function of goal achievement and the amount of change and prospects of change there are for Costa Rican society.

The Costa Rican political culture has been strongly shaped by the efforts and ideology of a single political party—the PLN. The *liberacionistas* have had the potential to shape the system, most particularly the bureaucracy, the great majority of whose employees are party sympathizers, into an effective operation providing modern decision-making methods to the society as a whole. Instead, per capita income, industrialization, diversification, and position on the world market are little better than when the PLN assumed power for the first time after a violent revolution in 1948.

Rather than concentrating on bringing change to the economy and society, the party has channeled its efforts into the shaping of a highly complex political structure, both internally within its organization and within the government itself. This entire governmental and political system is liberal and participant in orientation and moderate in its policies. The PLN has become a moderate, prestige-class party with the principal goal of keeping the Costa Rican system participant, stable, and liberal.

The political system of Costa Rica is formally equalitarian. All citizens vote, and proportional representation insures every vote a relatively equal voice in choosing representatives. Civil service examinations are required of all persons filling a post in the public administration. Education is formally available to all Costa Ricans. However, this formally equalitarian political system has served to reinforce many of the inequalitarian aspects of the society as a whole. The political system's problem-solving capacities have been limited by this formal equalitarianism. Participants in the decision-making process are limited and checked by others of their kind, while a great deal of overlapping responsibility occurs. Moreover, problems can be solved only when they are perceived as such, but the Costa Rican political culture tends to shield decision makers from many of the basic problems of the society. No far-reaching efforts are made to solve problems such as overconcentration of the population in one geographic area, overcrowded and limited educational facilities, the land tenure and agricultural production difficulties, and the nation's perpetual trade imbalance, to cite a few examples; for the systemic equilibrium so prized by the prestige class would be upset if these problems were tackled at all seriously.

The Costa Rican prestige class, with its pretensions, authoritarianism, and social attitudes, still has a more democratic approach to politics than do many of this same sort of class in other Latin American nations. And so it should, considering that this type of system has permitted members of the prestige class almost inevitably to hold down at least two positions while widespread underemployment exists among the working class. The system has permitted this class to permit formal political participation to everyone in the country and yet to preserve its position as decision maker for the society as a whole.

A FINAL WORD

"Pepe" Figueres, former president and PLN maximum leader, was selected as his party's candidate for the presidency in the 1970 election, and he emerged victorious. His continuing popularity insured that he did attain his electoral quest, although certainly not by the margin of victory he enjoyed in the 1953 election. Figueres is one of the few individuals in Costa Rica who might be able to reorient the PLN, put the party squarely behind an effort to bring badly needed change to the country, reorient and coordinate the public administration, and carry out an effective agrarian reform program. Unfortunately for those who favor change, Figueres and others of the PLN leadership seem to look to the past more than they do to the future. The *liberacionista* exploits of the 1948 revolution are more important than what the group will do in the future. Party leader Alberto Canas stated what may be a byword with the PLN leadership when he said, "Costa Rica has already had its revolution."[14]

[14] Personal interview, March, 1968.

Only the future will reveal whether Figueres is willing to risk the alienation of the Costa Rican prestige class and to implement strong reforms during his 1970–74 term of office. The chances that he will do this seem remote, since it is this prestige class that forms the very backbone of his and his party's support. There is no other individual with a well-organized party who could bring radical reform to Costa Rica.

The "democracy" that the PLN has done so much to create has gradually given way to a deadlock between administrative and political organizations, between agencies within the administration, between parties in the legislature, between the prestige and the working classes, and between the president and his government. Costa Rica's much admired democracy has contributed major stumbling blocks on the country's road to economic and social development. Because of its size and resources—human, economic, and social—the country cannot expect to attain the levels of prosperity and well-being enjoyed by larger, better endowed nations. But Costa Rica, despite its favorable position in the Latin American area, could do much better if the political system was capable of exerting more control over its internal structures, its environment, and its resources and could tackle some of the nation's more basic developmental problems. How long can a country, with a population that doubles in less than every twenty years, remain static?

Bibliography

BOOKS

Almond, Gabriel A., and Coleman, James S. (eds.). *The Politics of the Developing Areas*. Princeton: Princeton University Press, 1960.

Almond, Gabriel A., and Powell, G. Bingham, Jr. *Comparative Politics: A Developmental Approach*. Boston: Little, Brown and Company, 1966.

Biesanz, John and Mavis. *Costa Rican Life*. New York: Columbia University Press, 1944.

Busey, James L. *Notes on Costa Rican Democracy*. Boulder, Colorado: University of Colorado Press, 1962.

Castro Rawson, Margarita. *El costumbrismo en Costa Rica*. San José: Editorial Costa Rica, 1966.

Comparative Administrative Group of the American Society for Public Administration. *The Sayre-Kaufman Outline*. Bloomington, Indiana: Indiana University, 1966.

Cordero, José Abdulio. *El ser de la nacionalidad Costarricense*. Madrid: Editorial Tridente, S.A., 1964.

Duverger, Maurice. *Political Parties*, rev. ed. London: Methuen and Co., Ltd., 1961.

――――. *The Idea of Politics*. Indianapolis: Bobbs-Merrill, 1964.

Easton, David. *The Political System*. New York: Alfred A. Knopf, 1953.

Fernandez Guardia, Ricardo. *Cartilla histórica de Costa Rica*. San José, Costa Rica: Imprenta Antonio Lehmann, 1967.

Figueres, José. *Cartas a un ciudadano*. San José: Imprenta Nacional, 1956.

Garro, Joaquin. *Veinte anos de historia chica*. San José: Imprenta Vargas, 1967.

Goldrich, Daniel. *Sons of the Establishment: Elite Youth in Panama and Costa Rica*. Chicago: Rand McNally. 1966.

Institute for the Comparative Study of Political Systems. *Costa Rica Election Factbook, 1966*. Washington, 1966.

Kantor, Harry. *Patterns of Politics and Political Systems in Latin America*. Chicago: Rand McNally, 1969.

Lipset, Seymour M., and Solari, Aldo (eds.). *Elites in Latin America*. New York: Oxford University Press, 1967.

Martz, John D. *Central America: The Crisis and the Challenge*. Chapel Hill: University of North Carolina Press, 1959.

Monge, Luis Alberto. *No hay revolución sin libertad*. San José, 1961.

Monge Alfaro, Carlos. *Historia de Costa Rica*. San José: Imprenta Trejos Hermanos, 1966.

Oduber, Daniel, *Una campaña*. San José: Editorial Eloy Morua Carrillo, 1967.

Ortuno, Fernando. *El monopolio estatal de la banca de Costa Rica*. San José: Imprenta Trejos Hermanos, 1963.

Partido Libéración Nacional. *Carta Fundamental*. San José, 1951.

Pincus, Joseph. *El Mercado Común Centroamericano*. Mexico: ROCAP, 1963.

Veliz, Claudio (ed.). *Obstacles to Change in Latin America*. London: Oxford University Press, 1965.

Wilgus, A. Curtis (ed.). *The Caribbean: The Ceneral American Area*. Miami: University of Miami Press, 1963.

Zeledon, Marco Tulio. *La ODECA, sus antecedentes históricos y su aporte al derecho internacional americano*. San José: Imprenta Antonio Lehmann, 1966.

ARTICLES AND PERIODICALS

Almond, Gabriel A. "A Developmental Approach to Political Systems," *World Politics* 17 (January, 1965), 183–214.

Anderson, Charles W. "Politics and Development Policy in Latin America," *Midwest Journal of Political Science* 5, No. 4 (November, 1961), 332–50.

Denton, Charles F. "Bureaucracy in an Immobilist Society: The Case of Costa Rica," *Administrative Science Quarterly* (September, 1969).

Easton, David. "An Approach to the Analysis of Political Systems," *World Politics* (April, 1957), 383–408.

Edwards, Harold T. "Power Structure and Its Communicative Behavior in San José, Costa Rica," *Journal of Inter-American Studies* IX, No. 2 (April, 1967), 236, 247.

Martz, John D. "Characteristics of Latin American Political Thought," *Journal of Inter-American Studies* 8, No. 1 (January, 1966).

――――. "Costa Rican Electoral Trends, 1953–1966," *Western Political Quarterly* 20, No. 4 (December, 1967), 888–909.

Nye, Joseph S. "Central American Regional Integration," *International Conciliation*, No. 572 (March, 1967).

Pacheco, Leon, "Evolución del pensamiento democratico de Costa Rica," *Combate*, No. 15 (Abril y Mayo, 1961).

NEWSPAPERS

La Nación, 1967–1969.

La República, 1967–1969.

REPORTS

Johnson, John J. "The Latin American Middle Sectors: The Future of Reform." Paper delivered at Western Reserve University, Cleveland, Ohio, April 11, 1967.

Parrish, Charles J. "The Relevance of Comparative Method to the Study of Latin American Politics." Paper to the Southern Political Science Association Convention, Fall, 1965.

McGovern, Joseph J. "The Costa Rican Labor Movement: A Study in Political Unionism." Unpublished manuscript, Woodrow Wilson School of Public and International Affairs, Princeton University, October, 1965.

Smith, Donn Scott. "The *Partido Liberación Nacional* of Costa Rica: A Critical Study." Unpublished manuscript, Woodrow Wilson School of Public and International Affairs, Princeton University, October, 1966.

Worthington, Wayne Lamond. "The Costa Rican Public Security Forces: A Model Armed Force for Emerging Nations?" Master's thesis, University of Florida, 1966.

Index